LIQUIDATING
Life

Laura G. Cogdill

Liquidating Life

ISBN: 978-9891120-0-0

www.lauragcogdill.com

Cover Design by Elizabeth Babski of Babski Creative Studios, Tallahassee, FL
www.babskicreativestudios.com

Photographs © Laura G. Cogdill; John D. Cogdill

Photographs of reunion wedding pg. 53 by Phil Sears, Tallahassee, FL

Author Photograph by Polished Arrow Photography, Tallahassee, FL   www.polishedarrowphotography.com

Printed in the United States of America

<u>Dedication</u>

This book is a memorial to the valiant life of

John Dennis Cogdill

and to all who battle glioblastoma multiforme.

Acknowledgments

Enduring thanks and love to my family: Larry and Jonnie Ganus; Sharon, Bobby, and Marshall Hilaman, and the extended Hilaman family; my aunts, uncle, and cousins.

I am thankful for John's family: John and Gloria Cogdill; Tim and Jennifer Cogdill and their children Georgia, Kohle, West, Jace, and Raylan Dennis; Georgena Vaughn, the extended Vaughn family, and Dana Wellesley.

My dear friends were and still are a great support: Kelly Stanfield, Shirley and Vic Daniels, Gail Wells, Sarah McCarty, Ronnie Santeusanio, Cheryl Jackson, Rebecca and John Shaner, Kathy Cantrell, Joe Ann Houston, Carol Marchant, Linda Sarvis. And for those who "just knew," Pam Brasher, Fred Davis, Tawana Morris, Mike and Keegan Brennan, words weren't always necessary.

John's friends, customers, and colleagues were encouraging to him: The McKenzie/Gorniak families, Dave Fisher and Harriett Pfaffman, Danny Strickland, Tom and Marie Behm, Sandy Frazier, Larry Wolfe, Jim and Shirley Dollar, Jackie and Tom McHaffie, Harry and Suzanne Farrar, Mike, Pam, Terry and Lori, Eric, and many more he spoke of often. It was especially meaningful to have Bob Wolfe marry us at Oven Park.

Our Wildwood Church family was a constant firm foundation, especially Teresa and Tim White, Marty and Bruce McCall, Rae and Bob McClure, Curt and Linda Stine, Vicky Hayse, Sabrina and Arthur Grubbs, Pastor Bob Evans, and the Bereavement Committee.

First Baptist Church Havana took us under their wings. Many thanks to Dr. Eric Erskine, Matt Grieves, Bruce Power, Paula Moore, Joyce Causey, Walter and Ruby Watson.

Faith Funeral Home made an unfamiliar happening a peaceful experience. Their word is gold with me.

Once again, our friends from Amos P. Godby High School looked out for their own. Roger Day, Kim Harrington, Daphne McClain, Mitch Gans, and Marvin and Glenn Powell kept us laughing. My appreciation to Jordan Powell for video taping John, and to Doug Rogers for marrying us at our class reunion.

My Springwood Elementary family is priceless. Their love and support was evident, and it gave John great peace to know they would look out for me, especially after he would no longer be there to do so.

My sweet, caring neighbors, along with Bob and Betsy Bruggner, and Ginger Farrell confirmed my reasons for moving to a small town.

Thank you to the Tallahassee Writers Association and the Havana Writers Group for making me not only a better writer but a better person. Donna Meredith gave me the confidence to compile this book and over the last few years, has been a tremendous help in other writing adventures. Thanks for sharing your knowledge freely. Rhett DeVane helped me over hurdles of jumbled words, sprinkled with the humor I needed.

I will never again take for granted those who offer life-saving help such as the Leon County EMS; Tallahassee Memorial Hospital ER, Cardiac ICU, Neuro ICU, third and fourth floor nurses, and the radiation "microwave crew"; Dr. Gery Florek and his office staff; Dr. Christopher Rumana and the Tallahassee Neurological Clinic; Plastic Surgery of North Florida; Southern Medical Group.

There are no words to tell how wonderful the organization and people of Big Bend Hospice are. Our nurses--all hours of the day or night from in-take to end of life, social worker, and counselors have the kindest hearts for an incredibly sensitive situation.

I am eternally thankful to our Lord, whose Word gives me constant comfort and hope, and for sending John Dennis into my life.

***

There are a few tips which will help in the reading of this book. Some entries are written by me (LC), some are by John (JDC), and a few observations from my sister, Sharon, are included. I have tried to remain true to John's grammar and spelling as much as readability allows, showing the ups and downs of his language after seizures and in the eventual winding down of his brain.

To make it easier for those looking for help as they move through the experience of **glioblastoma multiforme (GBM), milestones, medical terms, symptoms, and supplies used** are bold.

In the early days of John's illness, there was much speculation as to what caused his first seizure and how to proceed. Because of the unknown, some entries in *Liquidating Life* seem inconsistent and contrary to each other. But if you read it in its entirety, the mysteries are solved and it becomes clear why some decisions and opinions were changed due to unfolding information.

Surgical biopsy/diagnosis of GBM until John's death was 16 months. Entries are marked with a countdown of those months.

Helpful websites are listed at the end of this book.

<u>May</u> is brain tumor awareness month.

<u>Gray</u> is the brain cancer ribbon color.

A portion of the proceeds from the sale of this book will be donated to brain cancer research and/or hospice care.

A Word from the Author

Each person represents a different life experience, some long and healthy while others seemingly leave this earth well before they should. We spend our time accumulating wealth, friends, and possessions that will be liquidated when our lives end. Whether the end of a life is expected or catches us unaware, nothing can prepare those left behind for the void created.

While every person who goes through an illness navigates it in their own unique way, there can be generalities, or common steps, others with the same illness can expect.

When John was diagnosed with a brain tumor, I was hard-pressed to find anyone who would commit to the finer points in the progression of the disease. The most practical information came from a close friend whose family member succumbed to the same illness. I held to her words: "At the beginning of the month he was good. At the end of the month he was gone." Every day John and I woke up, I told myself we had at least another month. I knew my theory wouldn't hold out forever and I determined no one else would be left to stumble down the path of **glioblastoma multiforme (GBM)** again.

Join in my trials, joys, and tears in an almost-daily account of the journey in liquidating life.

<u>The following is part of the tribute my sister, Sharon, shared at John's memorial service:</u>

One of the first things you'll notice is that some of us call him "John" and some call him "Dennis." If you met him before he was a business-owning adult, you call him by his middle name, Dennis. If you met him more recently, then John it is. Because his dad is also named "John," our family has dubbed them Mr. John and John, and sometimes, John Dennis.

Laura and John attended the same middle and high schools, and though they had friends in common, didn't know each other. They met at church in 2003.

It was easy to see they were two peas in a pod, attached at the hip, meant to be together. I often tell people that Laura and John were like an old married couple. Never in a hurry, always eager to do whatever activity the other wished, whether it be hiking, canoeing, checking out a state park, parades, bookstores, rides to the coast--truly enjoying one another. John soon became part of the fabric of her life.

John owned Angel Carpet Cleaning and was in business 20 years, with a loyal following. He worked hard and was proud of his business.

But then things changed on a dime. That fateful night in 2009 started a chain of events a year and a half long. You know how time goes. It seems to fly by. It all goes so fast. You look back and can't believe the day is over, the week has passed, and the month is gone. Yet when walking through a situation, time takes on a surreal molasses feel. It is thick. It is sticky, almost palpable, and tangible. You look back over it and see the thin, fast streak of time. But when you are in it, it is molasses.

John's perspective was always *his*. He never had fear. Always gracious in the face of the unknown. His sense of humor remained intact throughout, always cracking wise, even when the words wouldn't come out just right. Friends and family were John's world. Jesus was his heartbeat. His most heartfelt concern was for the people around him come to know Jesus as their Lord and Savior, cherish God's word, and rest in the salvation of the cross. We stand assured that John Dennis is now in Heaven because of the redemption of Christ. He was raised by a father and mother who taught him the love of Jesus and a desire to know His word.

PART ONE: FIRST SEIZURE

<u>August 31, 2009</u>   John Cogdill's update/LC email

Dear Friends,

Please forgive the impersonal nature of this email, but it is the quickest way to get this information to you.

Sunday night around 10:30, John called me at home, **talking incoherently**, using **made-up words** and making no sense. As we talked, his language improved and he could answer questions such as "who am I" and "what is the date." We decided I should pick him up and take him to the hospital.

On my way to his house, he called again, talking nonsense. I hung up from him and called 911. The ambulance pulled in his neighborhood the same time I did. When we got in his house, he couldn't tell us what day it was, where he lived--nothing. He walked out to the ambulance and when he sat down, had a **seizure**. He has never had a seizure before.

When they got him under control, I followed the ambulance to the hospital. He had one more seizure and **flat-lined** while I was in the ER room with him. He looked directly at me across the room then his eyes rolled back in his head. I ran out in the hall yelling, "NURSE, NURSE!" It was very surreal. They did a 'spinal tap' that came back normal, chest x-ray normal, blood work normal, CT normal. We spent the night in the little ER room. He slept fairly well.

This morning (Monday), they moved him to **Cardiac ICU** because he did have **irregular heart activity** in the midst of the seizures. They are doing sonograms of his heart, arteries, and more brain tests. They aren't sure if the heart stopping caused brain malfunctions or if the brain is causing other problems. They are probably going to put in a **pacemaker** to keep his heart beating at a regular pace because it now slows down to the point of stopping.

They found an area in the **left side of his brain that has abnormal or no activity** (I could've told them that!). He's having a brain **MRI** at 4:20 this afternoon.
His parents arrived from Daytona around lunch time today and are with him now. I am resting at my sister's and will go back to the hospital later this afternoon. I took today and Tuesday off.

He is alert today, but still **mixes up basic words** and I get to where I laugh right in his face because the word choices he comes up with are hilarious. The TV is a microwave and a book is bread, and his cell phone is a T. He's a hoot to talk with. After about 26 hours without sleep, pretty much everything is funny.

I haven't heard any test results since I left the hospital around 2 p.m. It may be a day from now, but I will give you an update when I know something new. Soon I'll give you the dramatic rendition of Sunday night in the ER.

<u>John's made-up words:</u>
beil-told = brain
uptart = paramedic
placehint = MRI
steertolin = doctor

<u>September 1, 2009</u>   John Tuesday/LC email
Not much new today. The cardiologist is still leaning toward putting a pacemaker in, but all the brain stuff has to be settled first. Once you get a pacemaker, you can never again have an MRI.

It looks like tomorrow will be the day all the test results come together for the diagnosis/prognosis. I'm going to work tomorrow, thinking if anything major is done, it will be at the end of the week.

Thanks for the good wishes. John is encouraged when I pass along your messages. He still mixes up words, and now has an **echo of phrases when people talk**. He said it's like a record album skipping for several seconds.

John's made-up words:
stuppyditey = tumor
unnersloss, t-lit, gatorstarts = ??
dealer = doctor

September 2, 2009   John Wednesday/LC email

I know this is a blow-by-blow but John's situation is so baffling to everyone. The pacemaker doctor just left. After talking with John and asking tons of questions, they are going to do a **"tilt table" test** to see what happens with his **blood pressure**. This will tell them how his BP reacts to his body's positions.

They will give him something to make his heart race and slowly tilt the table into a standing position. When some people stand too quickly, things go "gray" and the blood "rushes from their head." Some pass out.

She thinks perhaps his BP got so low his heart stopped. If it ends up being what she thinks, a pacemaker won't be necessary. They'll try to treat the condition with meds. They will then do a **TEE**, which is a camera down the esophagus to look at the back of the heart. Did you know they could see the heart from there? I didn't. They're looking for clots or abnormalities to see if a clot broke loose causing a **stroke**. Now they are saying he had a very mild one.

They'll do another, more specific MRI on his brain because the doctor who reads MRIs and his neurologist don't agree on what the spot is. One thinks it may be a **tumor** and the other says it's something to do with activity.

Tomorrow will be a busy day with tests again. John is free of many wires and other things that held him to the bed and he can now take walks around CICU (coronary intensive care unit) and take showers.

He'll be in CICU at least through the weekend. Thanks again for your prayers and wishes. As I tell John things he said and did in the ER Sunday night, he's amazed and shocked. Some were so bizarre they were funny. John is using words more appropriately today. He's made only a few mistakes this afternoon, but he still can't say catheter, which is my gauge for how well his language is proceeding.

P.S. I stand corrected! The nurse said it's not a camera down the esophagus for the TEE but a **sonogram**. I knew it didn't sound right to be able to see the heart from there, but she kept saying they were going to "look at it." It's been a long week.....................

September 3, 2009   I am still alive/JDC email
I went by ambulance Sunday Night. I don't remember anything after I got into the ambulance. I woke up in the ER and the next thing I was in the CICU department. I call this the Penthouse of the hospital. The doctors have just told me I had a small stroke and my heart stopped while I was in the ER. They are not sure which one cause the heart to stop. I am a little disappointment in no "bright light" experience. Boy if you want special treatment let your heart stop on you in the ER. Today is great and they think they have figured out what cause the problems. I am being put on medication today and Monday they will do one more test to see if the medication is working. I do have one more MRI to see if the spot in my brain is a tumor. If this turns out to be nothing then I will be free Tuesday.

September 4, 2009   re: latest update/JDC email
I have a little aftershock from the stroke, If you had a conversation with me you would notice the way I pause and substitute words. It is getting better but its still notifiable. I think I may get out of here today. Even the service is great I really want to get out and want to get back to work, This sitting

around is good for the first 24 hours then its real
boring. I never thought I would desire to sweat.
Thank goodness I have some big carpet cleaning jobs
waiting on me.

My nurses have been great. I know I am getting
charged for their services but I am already trying to
figure out what I can do to thank them.

I have become very independent. The nurses tell each
other about me is he really doesn't belong here. I
am the only one in the CICU that can unplug himself
and go to the bathroom by himself. All the nurses
are telling me they are fighting over who will get me
because I am the easiest to take care of.

I have an MRI this morning and that should be the
final test. Drum Roll Please!!!!

September 5, 2009 (Saturday)   email by JDC
I have been moved to a new room number. I am now out
of ICU but still on the third floor. I am still
having to wear a monitor to keep an eye on my heart
beat. I will be hear until Tuesday at least.

It looks like I am going to make it.

(later the same day) They want me to come back in a
month to have another MRI to see if the spot is still
there. If it is there they are going to talk about
planing a bio-mass {biopsy} to confirm if it is a
true tumor and if it is a killing type. Until four
weeks we want know for sure.

September 5, 2009   Friday night/LC email
John has moved from ICU to a private room and it's weird because
it's so quiet. Not busy like the ICU.

He wears a portable monitor but has to stay close by his room. He
is happy to be able to walk around more. I'm going by his house

in the morning to pick up more clothes and then heading over. His parents will be heading back to Daytona in the morning.

A high school friend stopped by the hospital and stayed until 9:30. We had a great time sitting around talking. He helped carry John's stuff to the new room. It was good for John to talk and use more vocabulary. I have noticed the more tired he is, the harder it is to retrieve some words.

Since the MRI was done so close to having the seizures and a stroke, they want to do another one in a month.

The second tilt test will be Tuesday. They've increased the **beta blockers** in hopes it will level out the heart issues and when he takes the test, he'll pass and be free to go home. John almost passed out on the last tilt test, which told them he has **neuro-cardiogenic syncope**. The general doctor and John's neuro doctor have cleared him to leave as soon as the cardio doctor says he can.

John's language is better and they say talking and reading will help improve it. Still can't say "catheter" but he has the first syllable down!

Several of our Godby classmates work at the hospital and it's been fun seeing them after all these years.

September 8, 2009   He's home!/LC email
Whew!
What a morning. John passed the tilt table test with flying colors. The medicine is having the desired affect. He said the difference in today's test and the one they did last week was amazing. No symptoms of passing out this time.

John couldn't get out of the hospital building fast enough! He even took out his own IV. (I don't recommend doing this.) We stopped at the grocery store on the way to his house and now he's asleep, worn out.

He'll go back for a brain MRI in a month and then a heart checkup in October.

All totaled, he had a stroke, 2 seizures, and one heart stoppage, one night in ER, 5 days in CICU, and 3 ½ days in a regular coronary room. Everyone who worked with us was extremely nice, caring, and answered all our questions.

Thanks for your support through this, although it's not totally over. His language is so much better, but when he's tired, his words come slower.

September 8, 2009   email by JDC

I had a stroke and they cannot figure it out. I was incoherent Sunday night and in the ER. When I woke up in the ICU they found a tumor on the left side of the brain and have not yet concluded if the tumor caused it or not. I will be going back in 3 weeks for another MRI. As it stands now I had a stroke and that exasperated my long held syndrome which cause my heart to stop. But when I go back for the MRI I may find out the tumor will be the cause of it all and then the real fun will began.

September 9, 2009   email by JDC to Laura

I am awake. I have lived my first day out of the hospital—wa whooo

(later the same day) Just finished eating and still alive. Took my medication and am fixing to take a shower. Trying to get this glue off my body.

I went walking to the store and did not buy anything.
Danny called about helping me do work and will call
back later. Been pretty active this morning and
still feeling good. Really anxious to do the first
job. May try and do a job with Danny tomorrow. If I
can help Danny when I am not doing anything I feel
like it would be fair to him when he helps me. Not
use to asking people for things.

Went to see my neighbor. He gave me a phone so I
don't have to buy one. He gave me two hand held base
units. I have one in the bedroom and one in the
living room. Phone will still be hooked up by
Thursday by 6 p.m..

Had some chicken and salad. Now I am tired. Really
did not sleep before but now that I have eaten feel
like sleeping. Think I will go try to sleep again.

September 9, 2009   email by JDC to friends
They don't know really what caused it. I seem to be
getting stronger daily. I have some good customers
and I really do appreciate them. I am amazed at how
I really am not worried about dying. I have gotten
all the last days worked out just in case.   I have
to go back to see if it has grown or is going to kill
me. I think if it has not grown they will leave it
alone but if it is threating they will be talking
about **biopsy** to see if it is a threat. That will be
when things get tough. So far it has been a 9 days
of getting better. Now I am just getting back to
normal a life as you can after a stroke and flat
lining.

September 10, 2009   update/email by JDC
my heart is still beating "Good night, Sleep tight,
and your dreams come true….."
Had breakfast and walked. Basically did not die in
my sleep. LOL

Land line phone is suppose to be hooked up today. I
am getting it just to dial 911 as my mobile phone
does not work well out here. Laura and I are amazed
my phone worked every time the night I called her.

Feel free to call me on the land line but just
remember I may not answer it.

Everything else seems to be going fine. I am still
dizzy when I move but the my medicine says it may
cause dizziness. What is driving me crazy now is not
being able to drive. Another neighbor has checked on
me and asked if I needed anything from the grocery
store, she won't go a day without making sure she
sees me. I've helped her a couple of times and she
is in worst health shape than I am.

I will check in later to let you know I am still
alive until then sing the song they sang at the end
of the Lawrence Whelk Show. Good Night

September 12, 2009   hey man I am alive/email by JDC
Yea a lot happened in a week. If I had not called
Laura (my girlfriend) I would of laid down to sleep
and not woke up more than likely. I had a couple of
seizures in the ER before my heart stopped and I
officially did not have a heart attack. My electoral
systems shut down was the best way the doctors could
describe it. I was the talk of the doctors because I
was the mystery of the week. I have a spot in the
left side of the brain and the doctor told me I had a
stroke in the side of the brain you talk in. That is
why I was incoherent when I was on the phone with
Laura the night I called her. I was calling my arms
wings and using all kinds of substitutions during the
stroke. I will be able to clean carpets next week
better but I may require a few days notice.

September 19, 2009   email from JDC to Laura
I am awake.   It was a rough night.   Thanks

September 23, 2009   email from JDC to Laura
I am awake and kicking

September 28, 2009   email from JDC to Laura
I'm awwwwwaaaaaakkkkkkeeeeeee!

PART TWO: SECOND SEIZURE

October 2, 2009 Friday   LC email

The ambulance took John to the ER mid morning. I met them there. They ran tests and all his vitals were normal. Blood pressure a little high but not bad. He didn't have a stroke. They decided the spot on his brain is causing him to have a form of **aphasia**. He understands everything we say, but he can't retrieve the correct words when he talks. If it's like the last time, it will clear up in a few days.

He already had an MRI scheduled for Tuesday. We're at his house now and he ate and is resting.

October 2, 2009   email by JDC

I am not having a stroke but I was in the ER again.
I am fine

Well I just went to the ER again. I had a brain
messed up and I am home now. Laura brought me home
today. Everything is fine and this Tuesday I will be
getting the MRI.

I am fine don't call me today I am exhausted and I
need to sleep. Laura will be over here tomorrow and
I will be fine.

October 3, 2009   email by JDC

I hope I get better. I am having problems reading.
I am not having writiing this. I am awake.

October 6, 2009   UPDATE UPDATE/email by JDC

News from Dennis' today
The tumor is still there and I will require **surgery**
at some point in the next 2 weeks. I will see a
brain surgery Oct 13 and will have to see a third

surgery to do the biopsy. I just heard from the
doctor's office.

So now we know

The MRI was today and the doctors office called the
same today and wants to see me Thursday Oct. 8th. The
doctor's office has already made an appointment for
another doctor for the Oct. 13.

It could be options:
If the doctor has terminal bad news then why would he
just call me in to say their is no way to help me.
If the doctor has no terminal news it is possible
there is a way to help.
I have no idea yet but it seems to me the tumor they
found is still there.
We will find out Thursday.........

October 6, 2009   Well my update/email by JDC
I found out I have a brain tumor. I will be going
into brain biopsy surgery next week or the week
after. I have already had two episodes since I left
the hospital. When the second episodes happen I
could not tell you my birthday but I did know the
president.

I know where I am but I can't talk very well. I am
very light head but can get around.

I will know more weather it is terminal after
surgery.

October 8, 2009 Should I shave my head or not?
email by JDC
Well this is proving I have a brain but there seem to
be an extra parasite. Unfortunately it is not extra
intelligence. While the doctor left me alone I
snapped a picture of the monitor screen of the MRI.
This little bug has caused sent me to the ER two
times.

It has **doubled in size** in 30 days so we need to move fast.

It is called a **cancer** but we do not know if its terminal. I will be going into surgery on Oct. 16. They will **drill a hole into my skull**, will find out just how hard headed I have been accused of being, and will take as much out as possible and send a specimen to the lab.

Once we find out how what kind of cancer it is, if any, I made need radiation or chemo treatment. Its still in the air.

The **risk** can cause some memory lost or blind since the location in the brain. So the risk is worth it. It will take 4 days in the Hospital and I will be back to work in 6 days. I have considered shaving my head before the surgery; send in your votes. I will video tape the shaving for your enjoyment.

October 9, 2009 Friday   email by JDC
I am awake. I still have the parasite.

MY TUMOR IN MY HEAD! LEFT SIDE

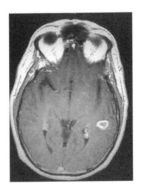

October 9, 2009   John's diagnosis/LC email
John is scheduled for a **left craniotomy** on Friday, Oct. 16th; time
TBA. He has a tumor in the **speech center** of his brain. They
won't know if it's **malignant or benign** until they go in and
biopsy it. While they're in there, they will remove as much of it as
possible.

He didn't have strokes, as previously thought, but **aphasia
episodes** because of the tumor. It has doubled in size in a month.

Starting tomorrow, I'm reserving all cell phone minutes for calls
only to and from family. If you want to reach me, please call my
home phone. I'll send email updates as timely as I can.

October 10, 2009   email to his brother by JDC
Since you are not going to be here, I know what you
can do for me. I would like to somehow send me a
video of you and all the kids saying Uncle Dennis and
wishing me well in my surgery. I could not remember
my birthday on the last episode when the paramedics
asked me when I was born. I will be making a video
before the surgery of myself because I may suffer
amnesia. I do not know how server it will be so it
would be helpful to have video of the kids talking to
me. Just a simple webcam from a computer saying
Uncle Dennis from the group would be good. Send it
email. Just enough I can see all you together saying
my name and that I am your uncle and brother

October 11, 2009   Facebook message by JDC
The one thing is my **apatite** has not left me. I have
no hair and some taste have changed but I still like
to eat. I get real weak if I don't eat. They did
tell me to eat small amounts all day instead of big
meals. I had my heart doctor tell me to eat "heart
smart" and I reminded her if I like it I was eating
it whether "heart smart" or not because I have very
slim chance of living past 4 years anyway. lol.

October 11, 2009   email to his brother by JDC
Well if things work out maybe we can all be together
at one of those Holidays. It may turn out to be my
last........lol

October 27, 2009   email by JDC
(after having his head shaved for surgery)
I am quit good looking without head..huh

October 27, 2009   email to his brother by JDC
The radiation starts next week. They have me on this
medicine {steroids} at double the strength and I am
starting to hear voices. I thought I was being page
over the hospital intercom but they don't have one.
I went up there looking for someone asking for Dennis
and they don't page anyone over the intercom. That I
will have to get use to. **Everyone** right now **talks a
slight octave higher note with reverb**. Its hard to
describe but I hear conversations in the back I my
mind **catches hold of certain phrases**. It will
sometimes continues repeat itself with reverb and
echo in my mind. Quit interesting. Thank goodness I
am not having conversations with the voices but if I
start answering them I have to worry.

I got the stitches out while in hospital and
radiology taken care of. I had a blast with the
people I had to deal with. This orderly and I who
came to take me down stairs had a blast. He brought
up a "bed" to take me who is dressed in full clothes.
I got under the sheet and let people think we were
dead. While on the elevator I blew through my mouth
just little. Man I could hear him trying to explain
it was muscle reaction. It was killing me to hold
from laughing. I tried to convince him to go through
the cafeteria with me in the bed to get a coffee. I
figured it was a drive through.

I told someone today I was going to be gone in 5
years but at least I don't have to worry about
climate change. I had people cracking up.

I am looking for a good night sleep tonight. You do
not sleep well at the hospital.
Love Dennis

[note: The night of John's first seizure, he was on
the phone with a friend. She facebooked him often to
keep updated. The following entry was one of his
responses to her.]

October 28, 2009   Facebook message by JDC
I know I was not making sense. I was barely holding
on. I had another seizer and went in the truck with
the lights on it. I didn't need to hang up but while
you were talking I was struggling to follow your
conversation. I thought I was going to bring myself
through it. Laura came over and had to call the
ambulance because I just about die again. That is
the second time I almost died in front of her. We
keep laughing it's often about you almost see some
one always die. Her first time was when my heart
stopped flat lined the machine in the ER.

October 28, 2009   Facebook message by JDC
I have all these miniature personal condiments
building up since I have been so many times to the
hospital. I can start my own Hotel. They give every
visitors their own small toot past tube, deodorant,
shampoo and three personal pans. I gave them the
number of someone who I usually give out for carpet
cleaning. I am about to work a deal out with a guy
who will work his and mine while I am doing the chemo
treatment. We will start Monday. If I was
independently wealth I could just live out the last 4
years relaxed until I died. However, I am not
capable.

The doctors have been real honest and I really
appreciate it. They told me the tumor was what they

expected and at the most optimistically I have is 3-4
years if the tumor response. The slim possibility is
past 5 years. I really am glad to have time to plan.
I am getting things ready now so those close to me
want have so much to do. It could be a lot worst.
There are kids up there who have not really expected
high school. I have already done all that.

The greatest thing about my situation dieing is my
world view. I have taken the last 7 years and
examined what I have been taught and found it to be
true. Christianity is the only philosophy which
makes more since compared against all the other
positions. I am following a logical and rational
position which Jesus the man/God taught was rational.
If this would have happened to me 10 years ago I
would have been on my knees crying to God to heal me
thinking I could convince him to do it. Now I am
content. With the teaching past down by the
inspiration through the Apostles (12) that allows me
to be content I will not die. My person will never
stop existing. When I leave temporarily my physical
body I am promised to return not only to my body but
with the Christ in His second advent. It has been a
great last 50 years because I found God is knowable
and He revealed Himself rational.

I was really happy to hear one of my friends said to
me. He said he wished he had the content I had about
my acceptance of dieing. I told him I wish every
follow of Christ could have what I have. However, it
is one of those things you want posses unless you
study the Testimony (the Bible correctly) God has
given us through man's history. The bible is the
most fascinating and impressed for those who read it
honestly.

I think this is why Laura and I both have so much
peace. It doesn't mean I can't be sad or mad about
the situation, but I don't waste time and energy
telling God how to handle things. I rest in him.

October 30, 2009   email by JDC
I am going to the doctors at the hospitals. He will
talk to me about the EKG of my brain. I will talk to

him of my medication. I seem to have problems
hearing people correctly, especially on the phone.

Danny is going to take me to the doctors and take my
van to do a job then come a pick me up.

You will get a weekly update as I know things come.
I will first up to date after the radiation and chemo
treatment.

(later that same day)
Doctor Chemo is changing my medication. I was
hearing music when no music is around. People are
hard to understand. I am having to ask people to
repeat stuff. **Being on the computer** is start to
bother me. I am starting to get **dizzy** some what when
looking at screen to much. I can still read thank
goodness. If there is a lot of noise around I really
have a lot contacting.

Reading the computer is starting to be a cause of the
seizers. Its not confirmed but I am getting troubled
by reading the computer. I figure I better stay off
the computer for awhile just in case I am. I will
send you any updates when I get them. I may have to
ask Laura to send them for me.

November 10, 2009   latest on John/LC email

We got the results of the brain surgery and it was a **malignant**
tumor, the "Ted Kennedy" kind.

John will begin **radiation and chemo pill** this Wednesday, 5 days
a week for around 6 weeks. He is feeling good and working.

He has several things going for him according to the surgeon: he's
young, they caught it early, removed most of it, and he's healthy.
The **life expectancy** for someone with "glioblastoma" is 4 years,
but not long ago, it was only a couple of years. If a tumor comes
back, they'll decide if they should do surgery again,
radiation/chemo; etc.

[note: the first night John took the chemo pill, he DID NOT take the anti-nausea companion pill because he thought he could handle it]

November 12, 2009   my first night of chemo..yuk/
email by JDC
I was really sick and Laura came over. I took the
pills around 9 p.m. and went to bed and woke up at 1
a.m. and was up every 30 minutes. My body was
basically rejecting it. I am fine now but I will be
talking to the doctor Friday before I take another
round of that stuff.

I have been through two rounds of **radiation** and it
only makes me feel bad for about 20 minutes after and
I can still get up and go work.

I have the weekends off from radiation but the chemo
I am suppose to take 7 days a week.

You really have to listen to these doctors. The
doctor in charge of the Chemo said I was suppose to
have my **blood checked every week**. They are dropping
my **white blood cells** and I could die from the common
cold. Then I will be in the hospital again for who
knows how long. I have my real doubts about this
chemo treatment.

15 months
November 17, 2009   one day it will be funny/LC email
This has been one of those really screwy evenings I might look
back on and laugh about one day. But not any time soon.

We had our parent writing night for all of first grade. I had one
parent show up. There were maybe 15 families represented in all.
It went well.

I took one of the teachers home. When we got in the car, my low
oil light was on. I've never seen it before so I was concerned. It
was running a little hot within a couple of blocks. I pulled in a gas
station to get a quart of oil from the trunk and put it in. I always

carry a quart of oil. But not tonight. I went in the station to bite
the bullet and buy some. I didn't want to risk burning up my
engine on the way. It was $4.39 a quart. But that's not all. Since
it was under $5, I couldn't use my credit card. I had to get a large
pack of Reese cups to push it over the limit. $4.39 vs. $2,000??
worth the lesson

We made it home, the oil light went off. I'll be running to the lube
guys tomorrow.

When I got settled inside I called John. He didn't sound very
good; said he was fighting having a seizure and couldn't talk. I
threw together my stuff and headed to his house. He looked fine
but was exhausted; felt like he does before they happen. He said
he had a little one before I got there but never passed
out.......hmmm......

John leaves his front porch light on in the evenings so the frogs can
catch bugs. Frogs my patootie.

I opened the screen door and stepped out. Something fell from
over the door and brushed the side of my head as it fell. I thought
it was a big moth or even a frog. When I looked down, an
approximate 10" anacondarattlerpython was playing possum at my
feet. They do that if they feel threatened. Tired, ticked-off woman
that I was, I took the rug and pushed it away from the wall and set
a double-sized cinder block on him. Ha!

I still haven't totally freaked yet. I was too mad that he actually
touched me. It was an oak snake. WAS.

November 19, 2009   email to his brother by JDC
It got worse and Laura came over because I did not
sound good. I really don't know what happened but I
had minor episodes I call them. Any way I have been
fine for the last couple of days. I am going to
start giving up the apartments because I mentally and
physically can not do them now.

I am one special person who is going to be radiation
on Sunday. The "microwave crew" is off Thanksgiving.
I told them they must know I have a good tumor in
order to pick me one of the few to do on Sunday. The
lady looked at me and gave me the, you sure do. I
really do something good when I do it. Lol

December 1, 2009   about radiation/email by JDC
about radiation: I know I am getting tired of them.
I told the doctor today if this is only for two more
years of life I may just cancel
now..............seriously   lol

December 2, 2009   email by JDC
I would suggest the first two books to read:

"According to Augustine, it is our duty to consider
what men or what books we ought to believe in order
to worship God rightly."

I like this because it requires me to use my God
given reason correctly in order to judge the spirit
which a man or book is purporting....

"How to Read the Bible for All Its Worth": Gordon D.
Fee and Douglas Stuart; Zondervan

"From God to Us": Norman L. Geisler and William E.
Nix; Moody Press. How we got the Bible. I have a
1974 edition but I believe you can find a newer or
like my edition on Amazon.

The first book deals more with _how_ to read the Bible
as _literature_, and the second deals with the
historical of how we got it and the _claims the Bible_
says for itself.

If you read these two you will have more respect for
how God has communicated to man (us) than you will
ever have experienced.

14 months
December 10, 2009   email by JDC
I am going to radiation and taking my Chemo but will
find out how much time I have left after all this is
over. I am about to head to radiation now. I have
19 more treatments and I go to work after treatment
so I am doing pretty good. I just get **tired at the
end of the day.**

I can't stay on this computer very long. It wants to
set off seizers.

December 29, 2009   email by JDC
About to finish Radiation tomorrow. So far I am
doing fine.

January 7, 2010   email by JDC
Thanks for all asking. I keep forgetting to update
Facebook.

Surgery was good the prognosis was brain cancer. I
have about, optimistically four years. Of all the
tumors you can get this is the worst you can get. I
keep forgetting how long it has been since surgery.
I am through radiation and Chemo and waiting for
another MRI which will tell how the tumor responded,
which will tell me about how long I to live. The
reacts were minimum to the chemo and radiation so I
was very fortunate. Was able to work as much as
normal during the treatments.

I will be getting off the computers and internet this
month because it bothers me more and more being on
it.

13 months

January 13, 2010   email by JDC

I can't taste anymore.....Wow

I still get hungry but I don't **taste**. I can
purposely chose to eat my favorite but I know in
advance it will be a strictly mechanical. This from
the "teleological" argument for God.

I can see things necessarily for life have pleasure.
I can enjoy food more than just a mechanical act.
Reproduce the earth with those one after your kind,
then enjoy teaching and loving them. Only this world
could have been conceptional or designed with intent
from a Personal God.

PART FOUR: SECOND TUMOR REMOVAL

12 months

February 17, 2010   text by JDC

Yes surgy. I figured since I already have clean underwear.

February 17, 2010   update on John Dennis/LC email

It has been another whirlwind couple of weeks for John Dennis.
The radiation/chemo treatments stopped at the end of December.
He had a follow-up MRI in early February and we got the results
Monday.

The **tumor returned** when the treatments stopped, and has grown
larger than before. There were several good options on how to
proceed, and John Dennis chose to have **surgery again**. The same
surgeon will perform the operation Monday morning. He is
confident he can remove a large portion of it again and start chemo
pills immediately so as to not give the tumor a chance to start up
again for a long time.

I will keep you updated by email. He isn't using the computer
much because he has a hard time reading and concentrating. After
surgery, this should improve.

Thanks for your concern, prayers; etc. I don't want to talk on the
phone right now. If you have questions, please email. I am happy
for him to take this option. If he did nothing, he would have about
6 months left. With surgery/chemo, it should be around 18-24
months. Repeated surgeries are an option as long as the surgeon
says.

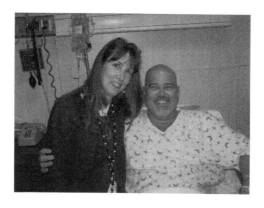

February 22, 2010 _____ surgery update/LC email

John Dennis' surgery went well. He didn't go in until noon. It's been a long afternoon. The surgeon got "all" of it. The tumor was large and **at the same site** as before. He's in recovery now (3:30) and will go to ICU in a bit, and will be there a few days then to a regular room then home. Chemo pills will start soon, probably 5 days each month.

p.s. For those of you I confused with my last email, John's middle name is Dennis. He went by Dennis growing up. Now he goes by John. I can always tell when someone knew him by what they call him.

February 23, 2010 _____ a little more detail/LC email

The radiation team will determine if one shot of radiation soon would help deter tumor growth. John will have a cat-scan in the morning.

This type of tumor **doesn't "spread"** like many cancers. It's a local recurrence.

We'll talk to Dr. Chemo to see how soon is "soon" in starting the chemo pills.

Every time surgery is performed to remove a tumor, brain tissue is disturbed/destroyed. Also, radiation destroys tissue, as well as the tumor itself. After seeing the effects of this tumor and a second surgery, the doctor said this would probably be the last surgery for John. They will re-evaluate if/when that time comes again.

He's been in quite a bit of pain tonight and can have morphine every hour if needed.

February 26, 2010   still hangin' out/LC email

John had a brain tumor removed Monday. He's in a regular room, not seeing dinosaurs anymore, but has some **visual field loss** on the right side.

He is walking several times a day and it tires him. All the doctors and therapy people are to re-evaluate him today (Friday). Hopefully, since he's not **hallucinating** as much (from **steroids** for swelling), he will go home tomorrow.

Chemo pills will begin as soon as the stitches are out (next week). The tumor either grew back during radiation/chemo last fall or it grew back quickly when treatments stopped in January.

(later that day)   HEADIN' HOME!!!!!!!/LC email

...in an hour or so.

March 1, 2010   John Sunday/LC email

John has had a **fever**, headache, vomiting off and on all weekend. Today I took him to the ER and they ran blood work and lots of tests and could find no infection, brain swelling; etc.

I'm glad they didn't find anything terribly wrong but he is still miserable. It could be a bug.

He'll see the surgeon Tuesday as a follow-up from the ER visit.

I go back to school in the morning/Monday. I am thankful his parents are willing to stay with him this week also.

March 3, 2010   what a difference a steroid makes/LC email
John Dennis' parents took him back to the surgeon today, who put him on more steroids. By the time I got to his house after school, his 3-day headache was gone. He got up and ate dinner, helped me figure out some of his billings, and walked around inside the house for about 15 minutes.

It's amazing how quickly he rebounded. Thursday we'll hear all the doctors' suggestions for the next course of treatment.

March 3, 2010   email from JDC to Laura
Love you   xxxoooxxxxxxx

March 4, 2010   This is short/email by JDC
After getting home Friday from the hospital I had to go back to the emergency room Sunday due to a fever. Not able to talk much and unable to comprehend too much right now. I am okay but having to have dad write this e-mail for me.

11 ½ months
March 5, 2010   LC email
John's latest vocabulary substitution:
German cooties = jury duty

April 6, 2010   LC email
John is having **surgery** again in the morning (Wednesday). The
incision site has not healed and has had **discharge** for a couple of
weeks. They will go in, see why and hopefully fix it. John has
been feeling well other than this.

I'll have my computer with me since it's report card time and I can
work on them online.

(later that day)
He has to be at the hospital at 8:30 tomorrow morning. I'm taking
him. John said his parents won't be here yet. I guess they'll be
coming up tomorrow. I'm going to email and find out. I don't
know what time the actual surgery is. John was very wound up
earlier.

April 7, 2010   LC email
Surgery is scheduled for 1:00. We're still in the holding room.
He's glad to be getting it taken care of. He's in a better mood
today than in the last few days since we know something.

(later that day)
Surgery was running late but John/Dennis has come through well.
The doctor took out unhealthy tissue, as well as the titanium plate
{from the surgery} and piece of skull under it. He will have a
"**soft spot**" where the plate and bone used to be.

There was a **superficial infection** in the skin at the incision site.
The stitches will stay in for about 2 weeks to allow the incision to
heal really well. At that time they will decide when to do chemo
pills again.

I asked what the doctor could tell about the tumor after looking at
the ct-scan Friday. He said it is there, but he doesn't know "how
fast" it's growing or how big it is specifically. An MRI was

already scheduled for the 28th of April, which will give more specifics.

He's in recovery now, will spend the night, and should go home in the morning.

April 8, 2010   LC email

When I got to the hospital, one of the **suture holes** had leaked. It's not the actual incision but where a stitch is in the skin. They are going to watch him and if the leak slows down or stops, he'll go home today. If it doesn't, they'll keep him another night.

John has slept since I've been here because they woke him up so much in the night, along with the combination of pain meds.

I asked why they took out the metal plate and bone under it. The bone was no longer connected to a blood source and neither is the plate. When they get infection in/on/around them, they are taken out because it won't heal. This suture area is having a hard time closing because the previous procedures/radiation have weakened the skin.

April 8, 2010   2:10 Thursday/LC email

John has slept most of the day. Around noon he had a tough time with extreme **pain in his lower legs**. They put the air-filled squeezy things back on and it seems to have helped.

The suture keeps draining and it looks like more clear fluid and less pink. He's had half a banana.

April 8, 2010   LC email to John's brother

Dennis doesn't like talking on the phone because it wears him out.
He hasn't talked to anyone on it since he came to the hospital. I'm
going home in a little while for the night. I had windows replaced
at the house today and will have to admire them in the dark when I
get there. Dennis is sleeping most of the time because of the pain
meds. I'm coming back up here early in the a.m. to see what they
think about the suture hole. Hope it stops leaking and he can go
home tomorrow/Friday.

April 9, 2010   LC email

The suture hole was still leaking this afternoon. They put **"glue"**
on it to seal it. He'll sleep sitting up tonight and they'll check in
the morning to see if it's stopped. If not, he'll go back to surgery
and they'll re-stitch it a little further over with better skin. He
hardly wakes up because of the pain meds. I finished my report
cards online today and have a substitute for tomorrow again. His
parents may come up if he has surgery tomorrow.

I don't know of anything I need right now other than spring break
next week so I don't have to take the days off. If his parents come,
they'll stay with him. If not, I'll see how he does over the
weekend.

(later that day)
John's suture holes keep leaking fluid. They are going to **re-stitch**
it late this afternoon (Friday). If this one doesn't take, a plastic
surgeon will re-stitch it yet again in a few days.
His parents will be here around 6 tonight.

The pain from the surgery Wednesday is lessening. They are
dropping his pain meds, but he's out of it most of the time.

(later that day)
The procedure is complete. It went well. The doctor said they put **extra stitches**, pulled, stretched, and did all they could.....thinks this will do it.....wasn't leaking after surgery. The nurse said they didn't want anything to get in through the leak and cause infection, or for brain/spinal fluid to get out. We hope this will be IT for a long time. Bet he has one heck of a headache.

Dr. Chemo popped in and said according to the ct-scan last Friday, the tumor has not grown from surgery in February!!

They'll delay his next round of chemo pills to make sure this incision heals TOTALLY. Chemo and steroids delay the healing process.

April 10, 2010   Saturday a.m./ LC email
John's parents spent the night at the hospital. Mr. John said Gloria wouldn't leave. They brought in a cot for her and he slept in the recliner. They've now gone to John's to see what groceries they'll need.

John is sleeping well. He ate some eggs, had gone to the bathroom several times in the night, and talked very well when I got here.

There hasn't been any drainage! No word on him going home yet.

(later that day)
The surgeon dropped in to check on John/Dennis. There is no drainage. The second procedure worked.

He's still groggy and having some pain. If he will get up and walk, eat, and come out of it better, he will go home in the morning (Sunday).

April 11, 2010   Sunday noon/LC email
John is more coherent today. Only one pain pill in the night.
Walked around this morning. Ate a little lunch. His doctor is on
the floor. Will know more later.

(later that day)
John is going home as soon as they can process his papers (12:30).

April 14, 2010   Tuesday/LC email
Saw John after school. He ate and bathed and walked out onto the
porch when I left. He
insists he had 3 surgeries last week. I can't get him to believe he
had only 2. Not sure where he's getting the extra one.

(also that day)
John is getting stronger but it's slow going. He's had a hard time
shaking the pain meds. The incision looks MUCH better.

I'm tired but catching up on my sleep. His parents will be here
until the weekend for sure. Not sure after that. Got my temporary
crown yesterday. Part of my tooth broke off below the gum. He
had to carve my gum. Not fun.

April 16, 2010   Friday/LC email
John's temperature was normal this morning (97) after being 101.5
last night. The incision still had some blood dripping. His parents
think he scratched it yesterday.

The surgeon was in surgery today but the office said take John to
the ER and the doctor would order some tests and come down to
see him when he got out of surgery. I talked to Mr. John (11:00)
and they were being taken to the triage room so we had to hang up.

(later) John went home around 3:30. He didn't get to see his doctor. They switched him to a different antibiotic and don't know why the incision is bleeding.

They did a ct-scan and I don't know what else. He got a written copy of the reports. I'll read them tomorrow.

John's temperature remained normal. He said yesterday, he and his dad stopped somewhere to eat. It was late in the day. He had iced tea and got chilled in the car. It went downhill from there because he was tired from their day.

We talked on the phone a long time tonight and he sounded "normal."

[note: We discovered that about a week or ten days after every surgery, John would spike a fever for a day or two. They could never find anything "wrong."]

April 17, 2010   LC email
Seven weeks and counting until summer!!!
John's pillowcase has some blood on it. To me it looks like normal after surgery stitch-yuck. There are so many stitch holes and they were very gunked up with blood, I think one or two of the scabs broke loose and that's what it is. He and his dad have gone out to do a small job so I haven't actually seen his head yet.

10 months
April 18, 2010   LC email
It's still dripping some.....a watery blood. He did pull a stitch loose but there are several in the same place. He's been out and about again and doing well. His parents want to leave Tuesday if he's up to being by himself. He probably will be.

April 27, 2010 _____ LC email
They are going to **leave the stitches in** for another week or two to
let it totally heal. He'll start chemo pills as soon as they can order
and get them in.

April 28, 2010 _____ NEWS FLASH/LC email
During my planning time today, John snuck in with a vase of roses
and a ring. He popped the question! The answer was "yes!"

_____ by Laura's sister, Sharon
Apparently John realized my sister was the best thing to ever
happen to him and he decided he needed to marry her. He wanted
to spend the last of his time on this plane with the love of his life
and concocted a plan to propose. Laura's co-workers and I were in
on it. I don't think I had ever seen him smile so much before that
day. Her first grade teammates called a "meeting" and John
walked in. They ate cake then divided Laura's students amongst

themselves so she and John could go downtown and get their marriage license.

The engagement was really, really short. Another plan was concocted. They decided since his parents couldn't come, they would have a private ceremony at Oven Park, a local park with lots of lovely flowers, plants, and a gazebo; just the two of them and a friend of theirs who has performed a couple hundred weddings. His wife took pictures. I didn't know she would be there, so I concocted a plan of my own. It was a weekday afternoon, May 5, Cinco de Mayo. I called one of my girlfriends. She put on a big, floppy hat, put her camera around her neck, and took out like a tourist. She'd snap a picture of a plant, and then sneak one of the happy couple. My friend rushed back to me with the camera and I rushed to the corner store to print the pictures. I put them in an album and surprised my sister.

May 6, 2010   LC text to John
Hello, husband!!
xoxoxo

9 months

<u>May 24, 2010 Monday   John surgery/LC email</u>

John went into the hospital Saturday night with **severe headaches
and disorientation**. The previous incision healed except for one
or two stitches. That area has **leaked air into his
brain/ventricles**, depriving it of blood.

Monday morning they will take out the old stitches, re-stitch the
unhealed area, and put a tube from his brain (out the top of his
head) to release the air. He'll be in the hospital most of the week.
His parents are coming. I'm hoping to work a couple of days after
the surgery.

There isn't a surgery time as they are working him into an already
full schedule.

(later that day)

Surgery is over! We're back at ICU for the night. I talked to the
surgeon right before surgery. John/Dennis was doing better today
and they decided not to put in the tube to drain excess air. His
body will naturally absorb it over time, and the ventricles should
refill with fluid.

The surgeon said they re-stitched about a 1-inch area that hadn't
healed. They haven't checked tumor growth lately because they
were concentrating on the air going into the brain. There will
probably be an MRI to check that soon.

He's resting well but with some pain. He should go to a regular
room tomorrow if tonight goes well.

[note: As soon as John was admitted, they coated the unhealed
incision area with an antibiotic ointment to plug the leak. By the
time of surgery, his brain had started to absorb the excess air,
which is why they chose not to do the tube.]

<u>May 25, 2010</u>   <u>Tuesday noon/LC email</u>
I am working today and John's parents are staying with him. They
did a ct-scan this morning and there is less air in his brain than
yesterday! We are headed in the right direction.

He has been in good humor this morning; no headache, but still
fixated on the cords connected to him. He's settled down a lot,
too, but is still restless.

[note: This weekend was one of the most stressful for me. Friday
night, my sister-in-law's mother, Georgena, along with Dana, and
Marshall, helped haul items from John's shed to my house in
preparation for a garage sale the next morning. Marshall spent the
night with us and during the night, I could hear John walking
around in the house, moaning. When I went in the living room, he
was stripped to the skin going in circles looking for the "big
water." The furniture cushions and pillows were all over the room,
and one loveseat cushion was soaked with urine. I walked John to
the far bathroom and he used it, got dressed, and lay down on the
dry couch. Part of my stress was keeping this weird behavior from
Marshall. Thankfully he never woke up. I tried unsuccessfully to
sleep on the dry half of the couch.

John slept until 10 a.m. Saturday. The garage sale went extremely
well, with participation from my sister, mom, nephew, sister-in-
law, and a disoriented John. I didn't realize he had no clue what he
was saying or doing. He held conversations, talked on the phone,
but sold his things too cheaply. Early Saturday evening, I
convinced him to go to the doctor, not saying "hospital" on
purpose, and John's headache was so bad, he agreed.

When we got to the hospital, he couldn't tell them his name, the
date, or where he was. In the ER room, he became more and more
fixated on the wires attached to his chest. After he was admitted
and put in the NICU, I went home, and returned Sunday morning
to find him in **restraints**. It broke my heart but I knew it was for
his safety as well as the nurses'. John was a strong guy with a
stronger will. He would straighten the wires around him into a
certain order, and when one would cross another, he'd slap the

bedside and start over. He also disconnected wires to put them in the order he wanted which caused endless beeping of the monitors. The nurse said he tried to pull out his catheter and IV and wouldn't stay in bed.

As the air in his brain disappeared, he fixated less. The brain is an amazing thing. John was totally functioning but had no clue what he was doing.]

May 27, 2010   Thursday a.m./LC email
Breakthrough! I spent the night at the hospital and when I opened my eyes, John was waving to me through the rails on his bed. He has talked non-stop since. **Doesn't remember** anything since Friday when he started feeling bad.

He's going home later and his language is much better. They're hoping it will get back to the baseline "normal" before this incident. There's less air in his head every day.

Chemo pills will begin Monday for 5 days, then an MRI in a couple of weeks.

Progress is wonderful.

8 months
June 19, 2010   fairy tale/ by Laura's sister, Sharon
The plot thickens. Laura and John's class reunion was coming. With encouragement from the planning committee, they decided to have a public ceremony on the formal dinner night of the reunion at the civic center. It was a surprise to the group. The families came and shared in the fun. Almost all the family. John's mom and dad were there and his brother's wife, Jennifer, and daughter,

Georgia. Georgia was the flower girl. My youngest, Marshall, was the bell-ringer. Our parents couldn't come because our Daddy had such a bad case of shingles. He was sick for weeks. My husband, Bobby, had to work because he had taken so much time off work with me because I had surgery the previous Monday. My oldest, Ross, took me in a wheelchair. We were a sight, but excited for John and Laura. They had a beautiful ceremony performed by a classmate who is an ordained minister, and a reception, obviously attended by their friends, with a beautiful cake, pretty flowers, and lots and lots of smiles. A reporter from the local paper was there and they ran an article the next week. It was a fairy tale.

July 3, 2010   LC email

Yes, John still has the **sutures**. I think he goes week after next for removal. He starts chemo again Monday. Haven't gotten results from the MRI yet.

July 5, 2010   tumor update/LC email
Dr. Chemo called tonight (6:30) to say the tumor has not grown.
John started chemo tonight and will do 2 more monthly rounds
then another MRI in the fall.

July 9, 2010   John surgeon appt/LC email
John's surgeon has referred him to a **plastic surgeon** for the one
incision spot that still hasn't healed. They want to see what he
recommends, other than re-stitching it.....again.

July 10, 2010   email from JDC to Laura
Medication is do love ya

July 14, 2010   LC email
The plastic surgeon is going to do surgery. John has asked for
Friday because he's entering his busy season, but the new doctor
wants John's previous surgeon there, too. They will have to
coordinate their schedules. At first John said no, he didn't want to
go through it again, but we talked about it more and he said ok.
They will make a new incision near the top of his head and pull it
over to the old incision.

7 months
July 16, 2010   LC email to John's family
Haven't heard from the plastic surgeon. If they can't do it
Monday, Dennis is going to wait until after the rush. He'll lose too
much business and both doctors agreed he could wait.

(later that day, after seeing the plastic surgeon)
After having talked with the regular surgeon, the plastic surgeon
thought the site would be much worse than it is. He was unfazed
by it; said it would be easy to fix. They'd make a new incision
near the center top of his scalp and pull the whole scalp over to
give the incision site new skin to work with. It's almost like they'd
turn it counter-clock-wise and not a straight pull. He explained it
better than I am.

Both doctors said it didn't have to be done immediately because
the incision is somewhat "together" but not solidly in that one area.
It does still drip blood every day, but neither doctor is freaked out.

Dennis asked to have it done today (Friday) or Monday because
we are entering his busiest season. Looks like that's not going to
happen. Now he wants to wait until business slows down. He's
doing great, working---but not too hard. I'm going to help him
during The Turn, sacrificing a trip to see the Yankees play Tampa
Bay (ha ha).

July 24, 2010   LC email
I think I'm finally over the bladder infections. The original
antibiotic wasn't the right kind for what I had. They discovered
this with the second bout.

John is doing well. I'll start working with him Monday because
it's time for the college students to leave. We are starting with a
sorority. It will take 2 or 3 days. Mainly I'm going to keep my
eyes on him. This will be my first summer NOT dumpster diving!
I don't want to have another garage sale. We've had two since
May. It will be hard not to pick up everything I see. I told John
I'll only pick up something if I have a specific use for it or it's
really cool.

John insists he's not going to let the plastic surgeon do the
procedure to fix the incision. It does look better but I think it

needs to be fixed once and for all. John doesn't want any more surgery of any kind. Can't blame him there.

I like being married to John and having him around all the time. I've laughed more in the last 2 months than in my whole life. We have a great time together. He now says we should have done this a long time ago.

My summer has been unorganized and busy doing silly things with John, which means I haven't gotten hardly anything done I NEEDED to, but it's ok. I wouldn't trade these days for anything. I have 3 weeks left. It has gone quickly. I can tell I haven't been on a trip because I'm antsy. Not sure where we'll go on our wedding trip. I'd like to stay within about 3 hours driving time. We even talked about staying at a new swanky hotel downtown for a weekend, eating at the most expensive steakhouse there, and do things we'd never normally do.

We're going to the church in our little town now. My cat is throwing up almost every day. The goop they gave him for fur balls helped for a while. Guess we'll be heading back to the vet.

6 months

August 23, 2010   LC Facebook message

Yes, I love married life. Can't remember what it was like before John moved in. We have a lot of fun together.

August 28, 2010   better/LC email

I must have a bug. Took a nap and feel better. Hope it's working its way out of my system now. Staying away from John.

I've been having small melt-downs for about a month when I
realized on the 30th, it will be one year since John's first seizure.
I'm not sure why it's so emotional; relief that he's much better,
one year of his life has passed, the emotion and stressful time, we
actually made it! Probably all of the above. This week I handled it
better and at breakfast today with some friends of John's (now my
friends), Dave, brought it up. It was a relief that someone else
noticed and said it first.

School went well this first week. I currently have 12 boys and 6
girls.

John and I are going to his parents' for Labor Day. He wants his
mom to experience us being there as married. I think we'll go to
Cumberland Island in October for our wedding trip. It will depend
on when he schedules the plastic surgery. He actually talks about
"when" now instead of "if" he has it done. The stitches from the
surgery in May are still in his head. It has to be dealt with. It
looks good and is sealed over with scab and new skin.

I've been feeling sick as a dog today. Don't know if it's a stomach
virus or something I ate. Feeling better now but sill a little
unsettled.

One year ago, John made that confused phone call to me,
followed by his first seizure, emergency room visit, ICU, and in
October, his first brain surgery.
What a year it's been; from the lowest to the highest. In some
ways it's flown, but so hard to believe a year has already passed.
Thanks for your support and prayers, and keep them up.

(later that day)
Home with John today. He woke up about 5:30 a.m. feeling dizzy,
clammy then cold and nauseous. I went to school and made sub

plans around 7:00 and I'm back home. He's sleeping. I'll wake him up in a bit to see how he's doing.

The new first grade teacher also called in sick with it. Glad I had it first this weekend so I know what it is with John.

(even later that day)
John has slept most of the day. He hasn't thrown up but is nauseous. Ate a banana and bread with peanut butter on it.....and lots of water. I may sleep on the couch to stay away from the sickness. Don't want it again.

It's been nice being at home!

August 31, 2010   John home/LC email

John is better but still not ready to eat or do anything. He walked around the house a few times (inside) before I left for school. His jobs rescheduled for tomorrow. I called them already. I left chicken and rice if he feels hungry later.

(later that day)
Talked to John and he feels human again. Ate a little chicken and rice and has been walking around inside and not feeling dizzy and queasy.

5 ½ months
September 5, 2010   Daytona Beach, FL

October 6, 2010   email from JDC to Laura
a wake me   xxoo

4 months; 1 year since first surgery/resection
October 16, 2010   nothing new/LC email
I went with John/Dennis to see the brain surgeon yesterday. The
purpose was to find out when he could have the **incision redone
by the plastic surgeon**.

When the doctor looked at the site and found out it rarely leaks, he
said we should leave well-enough alone and not fix it. I asked
what the gunk is over the stitches; scab, discharge, or built-up
medicine, and he said all of the above.

I mentioned that in the last two to three weeks, there has been a
decline in his speech and ability to process what's said. Could
this be tumor-related or effects from surgery, and the doctor said it
could be either one. And I told him there has been a glitch with
insurance in getting the MRI he was to have had in September and
I am very anxious to have one done. His office confirmed
confusion between Dr. Chemo's office, their office, and the

insurance company. The surgeon has ordered one and they are waiting for the authorization to proceed.

John and I have talked more about him not having the corrective surgery and he's not happy with the doctor's decision. After the MRI, we're to go back for the results, and at that time, John will tell the doctor his feelings about not having the surgery. He can't get that side of his head wet, and hasn't been able to since May. He has to wear a bandage whenever he goes anywhere and he's just tired of it.

We are waiting for an MRI appointment. **Chemo week is a little tougher each time**, but Dr. Chemo doesn't want to back off the high dose.

John's attitude is good, and if you've talked to him, his sense of humor is still intact. Not to say there aren't down days, but overall, he's a trooper!

October 24, 2010   JDC Facebook message
I can not welk [work] but can some.

---

3 ½ months
November 8, 2010   ???/LC email
John's MRI showed the **tumor has returned**. Not sure how big it is because we don't have the report yet. The doctor gave him **six months**. John's language continues to deteriorate and he has a **hard time knowing what people are saying**.

It's been a long, rough weekend.

November 9, 2010 _____ email from JDC to Laura
He cuty I have no

November 10, 2010 _____ LC email
Two men from our Havana church came by tonight. One is our
Sunday school teacher and the other is the youth pastor. John had
a great time talking Bible with them for almost an hour. We are
going to the old-timers lunch at noon Thursday. They want John
to come to it once a month if he's not working that day. I figured
we could go together and he can meet them.

(also that day)
Tim called John tonight. He and Georgia are coming after
Thanksgiving. He is going to try to coordinate the trip with their
parents.

I am also in a quandary about some details. John and I met with
his accountant today trying to put in order how to liquidate his
business. We came up with a good plan. John insists on being
cremated. I told him I don't like that. His accountant said FSU
(Florida State University) medical school takes bodies for
research, then the body is cremated and they give you the ashes.
John LOVED that idea. I like it because it would be for research
that might help someone else. Still don't like the cremation, but at
least it would be for a purpose. One of the men in choir teaches
there. I will email him to see if we can do it.

I decided to use Faith Funeral Home in Havana, but where to have
the service? John has brought up Wildwood Church in Tallahassee
many times this week. He likes Pastor Bob and even suggested we
could have the service there and a reception with Whataburgers.

November 18, 2010 _____ guess what/LC email
John's new word: pa-nan-ama = banana

PART FIVE: LIQUIDATING LIFE

<u>November 23, 2010</u>   First Entry Jitters/LC blog
Yesterday I bought a digital camera for the first time. Today I'm
blogging for the first time. Guess I'm finally entering the 21st
century.

It's also been a long time since I put thoughts into written words
on a regular basis. My goal is for my entries to be not only about
dealing with John's illness, but other aspects of life, too.

We started dating almost 8 years ago. August 31, 2009, John had
his first seizure, caused as we found out later, by a brain tumor.
It's glioblastoma, or "the Ted Kennedy kind." The average life-
span once it's diagnosed is 18 months. We're 15 months from the
original seizure, but I choose to think of it as a great year.

In February 2010, they removed the second growth of the tumor,
and in March, two incision revisions were done. May brought
another trip to the hospital because of air leaking into his brain
from the incision. Those stitches are still in his head.

In April, John proposed marriage. We were married in May and
June, and in September we celebrated our honeymoon by visiting
Cumberland Island, GA.

Chemo in November went well. The MRI found the tumor had
returned. When John pressed the surgeon, he gave him 6 months.
This started the conversations about cremation, Hospice, funerals,
and everything else you can imagine. It seems to help John to talk
and plan. Some days it drives me nuts. Isn't there more to life
than liquidation of everything you've lived? If John wants to go to
Burger King, we're going. If he wants me to keep my hair long,
that haircut can wait. It's pretty much whatever he wants.

In other postings I'll relay some from the conversations we've had
and decisions we've reached.

Hmmmm.........this wasn't as hard as I thought it would be.

November 24, 2010   The Day Before Thanksgiving/LC blog
Wednesday, the day before Thanksgiving. Thanksgiving should be
done every day. A **Hospice nurse** came by this morning for the
preliminary meet & greet, answer questions, and get us in their
system so when we really need them, we're ready to go. She was
incredibly nice and patient with all our questions. Of course, John
made us laugh several times during the dreaded conversation. He
is amazing. That is the peace that comes from putting your trust
solely in God.

This morning, John reminded me again for the millionth time the
most important thing is to know what God has done through Jesus:
given us redemption, salvation from eternal damnation/separation
from God. Only by accepting Jesus' death and resurrection can we
be saved from hell and be made right with God. Christ alone.
God's word alone.

About three weeks ago, we put our cat, Smokey, to sleep. He was
at least 14 years old and the best cat ever. Smokey had a large
mass in his abdomen that grew quickly in a 3-week period. He
could have gone through surgery and chemo, but I said one man on
chemo in this house is enough. He wasn't eating and had lost four
pounds; wasn't hopping on the couch with us or even onto his
condo to look out the window. We miss Smokey a lot.

I've researched the **process of donating bodies** to the FSU
College of Medicine. All donated bodies go to the **Anatomical
Board** in Gainesville. If you don't specify a particular location for
research, the body goes to the next open spot. We'll specify FSU.
The disclaimer says it can take two years after donation before you
get your loved one's remains. Two years is a long time, but if it
helps in the research to find a cure for brain tumors, it would be
worth it.

Tomorrow is Thanksgiving and the word doesn't even begin to be
adequate. (Does that statement make sense???) But you know
what I mean!

November 24, 2010   re: donation/LC email
After getting over the shock of it possibly taking two years to get
John's ashes back, I still think it's a good idea that may help
someone else one day. The thing that bothers me most is him
being "on ice" for possibly a year before he gets his turn at FSU.
And you know the call about his remains being ready will come at
the "worst time" as things like that do. I think I'll be okay. May
chat with the Hospice lady about it.

November 25, 2010   Especially Thankful/LC blog
Really, really thankful for so many things. It's been a good day.
Lunch with my parents, dessert with them and their pastor's
family, hunting, sister's family at dinner. Saw an armadillo,
squirrels, birds, and the biggest deer track I've ever seen. Now to
find the buck leaving the print. No early shopping for me.

November 28, 2010   Satisfying Saturday/LC blog
After being home with John for several days, it's going to be hard
to go back to work Monday. No headaches for him today. Yay

Went to my parents' along with Sharon to eat (again) and watch
the first half of the Gator game. Watched the second half at home
with John while I undecorated the fall stuff and re-did the mantle
for Christmas. Got a late start so I'll have to decorate the other
rooms a day at a time, especially with the Cogdill family due in
starting tomorrow.

Turned cold after a little bit of rain yesterday. John has always
been the hot one, but with chemo and some weight loss, he's
chilled easily.

We both have doctor appointments Monday, quite by accident, but
good for me. I'll drop John off then head for my dexa-scan. Just
realized I forgot to leave sub plans for Monday. Like I don't have
enough on my mind.........

LC email to John's brother and father
We're excited about the upcoming visits. Dennis is especially
thrilled to see the kids again.

I wanted to give you a few hints about Dennis for while you're
here. You've probably already picked up on some of this. If he
stutters a true stutter, not just delaying what he wants to say, he's
over-excited or wound up. Sometimes he tells me he needs quiet
and time alone to form the words, but with you, he may not. This
doesn't happen often, but when it does, it's obvious.

He has quite a few errands he'd like one of you to take him on
while I'm at work. Please don't drive too close to the car in front
of you. It makes him very, very agitated. Not sure if it's his **visual
perspective** or what.

A lot of **words are opposite**: hot is cold, Dad is Tim; etc. If
you're not sure, ask him again.

I'm not taking any time off this week. He wants to spend it with
all of you and I appreciate the help running him around. We'll
make a list and prioritize some things.

November 29, 2010   Marvelous Monday/LC blog
John and Dr. Chemo decided to **not do chemo anymore**. John
gave it the old college try: surgeries, radiation, chemo.....he's done
with it all. Dr. Chemo did give us information on another type of
treatment, but John isn't interested. I can understand, sort of.

Tonight we filled out paperwork for Hospice, the Anatomical
Board for body donation, **Do Not Resuscitate (DNR)**, and read
mail from the health insurance company. I'm mentally exhausted.
John got frustrated while we filled out the papers because he can't
understand it all. That's tough.

He has been so adamant about cremation. I still think donating his body for study will help someone else later. They would return the body instead of cremation, but that's too creepy, and I wouldn't want to see it after they work on it. I wish his Surgeon could be there for the study and learn what went wrong with the metal plate, see how large the tumor got, see the destruction radiation did; etc. Who better to learn from it?
Since his body will be donated to FSU, John tells people he's finally going to college.

I look forward to writing every day.
weird
I haven't looked forward to writing in ages. It's good to end the day in reflection and remembrance and leave it here. Saw where you can have your blog printed into a book.   good idea

Today I called the auto glass insurance fix-it place and they're coming tomorrow to fix John's van windshield. I also called Hospice and gave them more info to add to the file, wrote a letter to the anatomical board requesting his ashes be returned to us, went by the **funeral home** to meet and greet and find out what steps to take "at that time." Everyone we've worked with— Hospice, insurance, accountant, funeral home—has been nice and helpful and patient.

John is excited about the kids getting here soon. I think once they leave he will give up. He's had a good day; been right with me on conversation and saying words he hasn't thought of and used in ages.

Time for NCIS. We watch it every Tuesday night.

December 1, 2010   LC email
Went to the funeral home yesterday to do preliminary paper work.
I'd like to see him and John in a room cracking jokes about dying.
Don't know who'd win. John's body donation will be the fourth
they have done in the last year or so. He gave me the "order" of
what happens and when, like the Hospice nurse did.

Haven't heard from Dr. Chemo. John said he was going to call
me, and he will. Must not be anything urgent.

(also that day/email to a high school friend)
Dennis mentioned having your son video him talking about God.
Sort of letting Dennis ramble and you interjecting questions along
the way. It would probably need to be this month.

December 3, 2010   Friday Family Fun/LC blog
John's brother and family got into town late Tuesday night, really
Wednesday morning. Tim has taken John to run errands, to
Whataburger for lunch, and who knows what all. Big help to me
but most importantly, they are spending time together.

Enjoying being around niece and nephews and seeing John acting
like a kid with them. West, #2 boy, asked me if I was going to
keep living in my house once Uncle Dennis is dead. I told him I
was. His mom, Jennifer, says he's been full of questions. I told
him I'd answer anything he wants to know. [note: He didn't have
any more questions while they were here but he did give lots of
hugs. When John couldn't remember the kids' names, he'd call
them their birth-order number.]

Tonight we ate dinner at Jennifer's mom's, then Tim, Jennifer,
John, and I went to high school friends' for coffee, cookies and
queso. We had a great time. John had a hard time keeping up with
the quick-moving conversation. When we got home and he told
me what he heard, he was right on it for the most part.

Tomorrow, John's parents are coming from Daytona for a week or so. They'll be staying with us. I'll probably be going with Sharon and Marshall to the Christmas parade downtown tomorrow night. Always fun and will give John and his parents some time to get caught up.

December 7, 2010   LC blog

It's been a fun, exhausting, emotional, busy week with Tim and Jennifer and the kids here, along with John's parents. Last night we had a delicious steak dinner at Jennifer's mom's and reality finally hit me in the face when it came time to go home. Tim's crew was leaving for Idaho the next morning, and I realized Tim would probably never see John again. The realization dangled around as we took family pictures and silently overtook us when we started giving good-bye hugs.

Jennifer's mom had her back to us doing dishes when we came in to tell her thank you again and give Jennifer hugs. When her mom turned around, her eyes were filled with huge tears. That's when we all lost it. John, of course, was the strong one. He laughed it off saying we were girlie girls or something like that.

Tim met us at the car and couldn't talk. They shared I love you and hugs. A couple of people stood on the porch and watched from a polite distance. It was surreal. That's the only word I can call it.
surreal

John's parents took him to the surgeon today because of a **walnut-sized bulge** under the incision. They'll do a ct-scan tomorrow. The debate is whether it's tumor coming out or infection. Good grief.

We've gotten paperwork signed and witnessed for Hospice, the funeral home, anatomical board, will, POA (power of attorney), DNR, and a bunch more. John's family has been a big help hauling him around last week and this. He said today when he handed me all the papers, "I'm ready to go now."

And he is. I'm not ready for him to go, though.

December 8, 2010   chilly willy Wednesday/LC blog
Dr. Chemo **doubled the steroid** Monday, and today, John has been wound up, and this evening, hearing bombs. Not sure if he's hearing actual explosions or the word "bomb" in conversations. He watched the news with his parents and when a talk show came on, he thought they were still talking about the same things as on the news: internet, bombs, bombs. everything was bombs When he realized we weren't being bombed, he calmed down some. He went to the bedroom and lay down until his parents went to bed. He came to the living room where I was. Kept the TV muted and now he's napping.

Will be going to town hall to **reserve cemetery plots** next week. Exciting, huh?

December 9, 2010   curiouser and curiouser/LC blog
It gets more curiouser and curiouser. The bulge under the incision of John's head is the **tumor protruding**. They took out the area of skull where they originally did surgery. Instead of growing "in" the tumor is growing "out" and pressing against the skin.

He isn't in pain unless you press that area. It looks like half a walnut under the skin. His prognosis hasn't changed....6 months, and this weird growing pattern has actually bought him a little more time since it's not totally inside his brain wreaking havoc. Since the **doctors aren't treating him anymore**, we're on Hospice's radar and they can help when we need it.

He went for an hour and a half walk when we got home today, ate, and went to bed.

His whole family just left after being here for over a week and it was great for him to have them around. John is at peace with the end of life. I can't imagine what it's like to be him right now, although he's almost excited to meet God face to face and have all his theological questions answered, and be able to talk and read and teach in heaven. His main concern is that people remember/learn what Christ has done for us.
Can't add anything to that.

December 11, 201   casteerdia/LC blog
casteerdia
Reminds me of stuppeeditey. John's made-up words.
Today was weird. Mama and I went shopping this morning, and when we got home, John was lethargic and feeble. We walked uptown, came home, and he rested. Then we went to Burger King. While we were there, he asked me what gifts I remembered him giving me over the years. Talk about putting a girl in the hot seat. But he gives great gifts, and Sharon and I had this conversation the other day. I reminded him of the footie/camo pajamas, teddy bears, turquoise bracelet, and Yankee jersey. He remembered a couple of necklaces, and the perfume "he" got from Victoria's Secret......Sharon really picked up the perfume for him. He laughs when he talks about it. He didn't want any help with the bracelet and was proud of what he got. We talked about a few other things and places we'd been. I wanted to come home and look through pictures for more memories, and we did.

Later, John perked up. He said his **head had been hurting** earlier and he knew he was acting weird. We watched Andy Griffith at 7 p.m. Had to mute the sound because John kept "hearing" them talk about catastrophes. He was rational enough to know they weren't, but asked me to make sure.

John's friend, Dave, called from Atlanta, and John told him bye and how much he has enjoyed knowing him. It was bittersweet. Quite a few of his friends have called lately and it's meant a lot to John. Don't think he knows I've emailed many of them with the latest update. He's determined to be "gone" by the new year and after watching him today, when he gives up, it will be over.

I'm craving noise. John **likes it quiet** and as long as we've been married, he can't handle extraneous sounds like background radio/TV/movies. I like something quietly going in the background usually, but can do silent also. But lately, there is nothing in the background so my head is empty. (ha ha   bad choice of wording)

December 12, 2010   more liquidating/LC blog
Today as I dressed for church, I put on the beautiful poinsettia pin John gave me a few years ago. Another wonderful gift from a wonderful man. He remembered the pin and the story: we passed a stand of brooches as we left a department store one day. This one caught my eye; beige/brown swirled cloisonné on the petals, burnt orange jewels in the center. I only mentioned in passing how much I liked it and was surprised when I opened the box that Christmas.

Yesterday I picked up a carpet cleaning supply catalog a friend had borrowed. John has tried to inventory his equipment but **needed pictures** because he **can't remember the names** of items. He went through the catalog and circled what he has. Today we wrote it all down with current prices, for prospective buyers. Really need the business to sell before the end of the year.

We have many activities this week: three parties on different nights, but I will probably go to only one. John sits home all day and I can't go out and leave him alone at night. He **can't take the noise, movement, and commotion** of groups, so he won't go with me. It's okay. I'll have other parties later. I want to be with him right now.

Last week of school before break. Can't believe it's already here. It's been a fast first semester. The good ones go too fast.

December 13, 2010   mixed up Monday/LC blog
It was a weird day for John. When I called him at almost 2:00, he
said he had just gotten up. Then I remembered I made coffee for
him before I left. Didn't worry too much because the maker cuts
itself off after a while. Seems he got up as usual, put together my
students' Christmas goodie bags, washed dishes, was worn out,
laid down, had a sinus headache, took a pain pill, and it knocked
him out. When I got home around 5:00, he was still in bed. He
got up, ate, talked a lot, and went back to bed. He's up now at
10:30. We'll see how long it lasts.
The incision is dripping some. Has a **"pocket" of fluid** at the
bottom of it. I'll call and tell them tomorrow.

That was quick. Already back in bed. I'm getting together
information for a prospective buyer of the business. Man, I hope it
happens and quick. It would be a huge weight off John.

December 14, 2010   LC email to John's brother
Yesterday was kind of weird. Seems the cold plus the pain pill
was too much. He said he probably didn't need that kind of pain
pill after all. I've cut them in half yet again since they're so strong.

He said when you call, it's hard for him to tell you what he's been
doing all day. He'd like to talk about things you did as
kids/teenagers. "Remember when we......" he said. And he wants
to hear about what his name-sake is doing...... "but I know he's
good looking because he's Dennis like me."

December 15, 2010   interview
LC email to high school friend
I can't tell you how exited Dennis was when I told him about your
email. Can we video next week when I'm home from school?

Your son probably doesn't understand the magnitude of what he's
embarking on. Dennis said this is his last chance to tell people

what Christ has done. He wants to show the covers of a few of the books he's read and give a little info on them. I think in the flow of his talking, questions will arise, like at the hospital when you visited, and your main problem will be stopping him. He will probably cry some because this is dear to his heart and he knows it's his last venue to tell it. Christ alone is the only way to God. Faith means trust. It's not a "force" to get what you want.

I'm speechless at how our friends have gone above and beyond to help us in so many special ways. Dennis is enjoying guys coming to visit. He said he **isn't going out to eat** anymore. It's too **confusing**.

December 15, 2010   whirlwind Wednesday/LC blog
The **Hospice nurse** came to the house for the first official visit. Mama was there with John so I could work. Answered a lot of questions about insurance. John's insurance will cover 38 days of Hospice. The Hospice people are helpful and will work with you however they can. John needs a better bandage to cover the incision and they are going to find something. I love the term "tuck-in" nurse. Sounds comfy cozy. She calls at night to see if you need anything. There's also his RN who is available for questions or services.

John was "tickled pink" that the **admissions nurse** came back again today and gave us his patient number and answered more questions. Gives him great peace of mind.

The tumor doesn't seem to have grown any today and hasn't leaked in two days.

Santa walked past my classroom on his way to kindergarten for their parties, and the debate began.........is he real or not? As always, there are strong opinions on both sides. I think in the end, they all hope he's real.

December 16, 2010   LC email to John's brother
Dennis said he doesn't want a webcam because he **can't work the computer** much anymore and when he does, it exhausts him. He likes seeing your pictures on Facebook when I show him and seems satisfied with that and your calls.

December 17, 2010   thrilling Thursday & failing Friday/LC blog
Thursday, a friend brought lunch to John. When I got home, he was dressed in a blue shirt and jeans. He looked handsome. First time he'd dressed in a week, was wound up and full of energy. I asked him where lunch came from. He thought for a second and went, "moo." I knew immediately. Chick-fil-a.

After our friend left, Mama brought a chicken pot pie and Congo bars (a must-have for chocolate lovers). It was a very good, encouraging day.

During the night, John woke up and **couldn't go back to sleep**. Around 3:30 he took an over-the-counter P.M. I knew when I got up for work he'd still be zonked. He told me "good night" when I left. I called during the day and he sounded okay but not as chipper as yesterday. When I got home, he **hadn't dressed** and was **tired**. He was glad no one had come over. His childhood friend called and is coming tomorrow around lunch time. John is happy he's coming. Loves talking about God with him because he always has lots of questions.

The **incision looks much bigger** today. It looks like it's spreading wider, not just poking out more. You can see the **stress of the stitches**. A day at the time. A day at the time.

Usually John goes to bed before me because I'm the night owl. Tonight he was again in bed and I said something about coming in later. He said, "Yea, after I'm asleep. I'd like to fall asleep holding you once in a while." How can you deny that request??? I put on my pajamas. He was surprised. I told him I'd get up and finish what I was doing after he fell asleep. He laughed. And I did get up. I can tell when he's asleep because his fingers and hands twitch. He also made a snarling face a few times. Don't know if he was dreaming or his sinuses were bothering him. We've both had a cold for a couple of weeks.

2 months
December 19, 2010   perfect present/LC blog
John and his friend were eating wings when I got home from the mall. I left them talking and walked around downtown Havana for a while. It was drizzling, cold, windy, and depressing. The Christmas music was slow and an unexpected downer.

John went to bed about 7:30 p.m. which meant he woke up around 2:30 and couldn't go back to sleep. He **walked laps** inside the house until he wore himself out and went back to bed. His morning was emotional and weepy. He was still tired and the **incision had leaked yellow** again.

I never know what to expect with John because he is like a kid when it comes to gifts. He gave me my Christmas present after we finished breakfast. It was an enlargement of a picture I took on our honeymoon to Cumberland Island in September.

A little back-story and explanation:
When we decided to get married, my friend, Kelly, gave us bride and groom rubber duckies. I sent them on a honeymoon to Kiev with a friend during spring break. They ride in my car, were at our wedding at Oven Park, and went on our honeymoon to Cumberland Island. John made fun of me taking their pictures with horses in the background, at the Dungeness ruins, on the rail of the dock where we caught the ferry to the island--the picture he chose for my present. He wanted a gift that was personal to us, and saw the picture on his computer recently. "You've had them with us all the time," he said. No one else would "get it" but we do. Well, family and a few close friends know about the ducks.

We're putting a gauze pad over the tumor and using an ace bandage to wrap around John's head to keep the pad on. The sticky bandages don't work anymore, partly because the tumor is big, and partly because a bigger pad is in his hair and pulls when I take it off. He feels more secure with the ace. Today the gauze had quite a bit of yellow drainage on it, and the incision had a nickel-sized dried yellow glob of drainage. John wants me to call the Hospice nurse tomorrow. Not that they need to visit, just let someone know. Not sure if it's brain fluid or infection.

The preacher's sermon this morning was on how Jesus gives life. Ironic on the surface, if you took it to mean only a fuller life on earth. I remember what John is always telling me, "I'm not really dying. I'll be alive forevermore with Christ, which is the life Jesus gives. Eternal life in him." I found my mind wandering to death certificates and how many copies I'll need.

Have a list of errands to run tomorrow so I can be home (!) the rest of the holiday/vacation.
perfect

December 20, 2010   errands, naiveté, and meltdowns/LC blog
Ran lots of errands today, saw friends, made phone calls, met
Hospice social worker, cousins came over to bring food. Makes
me wonder how I work and get anything else done.

John was his usual jovial self while the social worker was here. He
asked if this was John's typical demeanor. "Yes," I said. "He's a
laugh a minute." By the time the session was over, John and I
were so stressed, we almost had our first fight. He says I don't tell
him things I do, that I make decisions and have conversations with
people and don't tell him. I do keep him informed. He truly
doesn't always hear or understand me. What he was mad about
was getting on **disability**. I haven't told him anything about it
because I haven't gotten it done yet. It seems to be the "one thing
too much." We have the **letters from his doctors** to go with the
application. After we talked and got it clear, we cried. It was a
stressful afternoon. I'm glad I'm home with him these two weeks.

The Hospice nurse will be visiting for the first time tomorrow
morning. Our **"team"** has gone out of their way to see to our
needs.

The tumor bulge has a **spot that drips** blood. I think it's where a
stitch is. We hope the nurse can make sense of it and help us
bandage it better. The ace didn't work too well because in the
night when John would roll his head, it would slip off. Now he's
using an old stretchy **headband** of mine. I told him he looks like
he's ready to run a race in a sweatband from the 1980's.

Tomorrow, one of the management companies John has done tons
of work for is bringing dinner/lunch/food. I'm **learning to
receive**.

December 21, 2010   nothing in life is free/LC blog
A substitute Hospice nurse brought bandages. She was shocked at
John's tumor/incision site and is letting the doctor know it's
leaking yellow and has one spot dripping blood.

Last night John had **trouble getting off the couch** but today he's been very mobile. Right **arm, hand, and leg are getting weaker**.

The management company brought a feast today. Thankful for everyone keeping us fed.

Today was warm and sunny. We went walking in the street twice. Our neighbor who also battles cancer met us on her walkway. We're all taking one day at a time.

December 22, 2010   LC email to John's brother and father
I know Dennis called you both tonight and I wanted to interpret. Hospice has visited the last three days, getting **baseline** information, bringing bandages; etc.

Yesterday was a change. When trying to get off the couch twice and getting up from the kitchen chair, Dennis couldn't get up. His legs couldn't do it. I let him pull on me and he balanced on the coffee table in the living room.

This morning, he bounced out of bed and hasn't had a problem getting up and down. He is a little **wobblier when walking**, and his right arm, hand, and leg are weaker. He's **lost** a little more **vision on the right side** and is being more careful when walking.

December 22, 2010   wild Wednesday/LC blog
All of the sudden I have 19 posts. How did that happen? Have I written that much? Have at least 19 days passed since I began this blog? Time is going too fast.

Today was BUSY, busy. One of our friends from high school came over this morning and brought his son, the aspiring film school student, to record John talking about his beliefs. We waited a week too long to do this. Last week John could still talk my head off about God and apostles and details, but this week, he's **lost more language and comprehension**. The filming lasted almost an hour and a half. A lot of it was repetitive, but he got across the main points: all you need to know about God is in the Bible, Jesus and his sacrifice redeem us from sin, it's our responsibility to study the Bible. It's his trust in God and knowing he's redeemed by Christ that gives John the peace to be ready to die. "I hate to say it but I'm looking forward to going." It is all-important for John to leave behind writing and video of his sharing God's message.

After these friends left, we ate lunch. John rested and Mama came over. The Hospice social worker came back with more information on insurance in the coming year. John will be responsible for paying his health insurance deductible again at the beginning of the year until it is met. His insurance's end-of-life care will only cover about 38 days, which began at the time of admission to Hospice.

A guy John worked with for years came by with his baby girl. She is a doll. They sat in another room and visited and played with the baby while Mama and I talked with Hospice. It was a good diversion for John.

Talked to a couple of friends and family today. It's great to be off work. But.......I find myself **frustrated** with John from being around him all day and night, mainly because he gets ornery if decisions are made that he doesn't understand. He still doesn't want me to get him on disability, and when we talk about it, we fuss because we see it differently. Sometimes I want to throw my hands up and say "whatever" but I let it go and try again later. I can see clearly when he's tired and should lay down, but he fights it because he doesn't want to be up all night. That's when he gets really **irritable**. But all in all, there's not much to complain about. He's handling everything well and for the most part, does listen to what I say. Maybe I'm tired and don't realize it.

Tried to talk to John's health insurance company today but they won't tell me anything because I'm not attached to the policy.

Tomorrow I'm faxing a **durable POA** so they can tell me what the policy covers and doesn't cover, costs, co-pays; etc.

Another warm day. We walked a little, and John went out by himself to walk twice. The Bradford pear tree outside our windows is a spectacular umbrella of yellow, gold, orange, red, and every color in between.

December 23, 2010   brilliant idea/LC email to John's brother
Dennis is on the phone with his niece right now. He has waited all morning for her to call. If she can call again, it would be great. He's telling her about all the food people have brought over and people that have visited. She is gracious to listen and try to understand.

Thanks because Dennis was bored today. No visitors. Guess I'm boring.

December 23, 2010   I'm bored out of my mind/LC blog
John's favorite saying today.....I'm bored out of my mind. Can't read, can't write, can't keep up with conversations on TV. He took out some of his Bible commentary books and looked at the pictures in them. I asked if he **remembers the stories when he looks at the pictures**. He said pretty much, and pointed to a map of Israel and a particular place on it. He remembers that Paul and Jesus spent time there, and in his head, he can recall this and loves those stories. The sections of the book had large headings and I asked if he could read them. Yes, in his head but not out loud. The brain is an amazing thing.

John looking at the pictures reminded me of a 10-volume set of Bible story books stored in the attic. They have several pictures for each story. I brought them down and John is enjoying looking at them. He asked me to find a few specific stories and we marked them.

We played checkers and I finally beat him! Mama was our only visitor, and only because she left her jacket yesterday. John's niece called. He knew she was going to because his brother told him yesterday. John got up expecting a call. With the two-hour time difference, I wasn't sure how "early" it would come, but around 11:00 our time, I heard the phone ring and him say, "Oh, goodie." They talked for a long time. The highlight of his day. We took pictures of ourselves under the gorgeous Bradford pear tree. He wants the kids to see the beautiful colors of the leaves because evergreens covered in snow are all they have now.

John and I changed his patch tonight and I think the tumor area is not as protruding. I mentioned it to him and he said "good. Maybe it's growing in now and it will end." I rolled my eyes at him. I know what he means but don't like it. He got around well today. Would do an activity and then rest, do another activity and rest. He stayed up until 10 p.m. and is snoring in bed now.

Talked to the accountant and lady who is buying the business. Told them to talk amongst themselves because it's stressing me too much to deal with business-selling language I'm not familiar with. I trust him to make sure the paperwork is correct and to keep her protected. I'm sure once it's finalized, John will be at peace that everything in his life is complete and it will be the true beginning of the end.

John had me buy him **pull-up protective underwear** today. He doesn't need them yet, and Hospice will give them to us eventually, but he doesn't want his first accident to be at my parents' when we spend the night there for Christmas. He thinks of everyone and every thing. I've never purchased them before and wasn't sure what size to get. He hasn't tried them on to see how I did.

December 24, 2010   Christmas Eve/LC blog

Last night was awful. John woke up about 2:30 a.m. and **couldn't go to sleep**. He went to the couch, which didn't help, so he started his laps inside the house.

He had taken ibuprophen or a P.M. or something around 12:30 and didn't want to take anything else. I walked laps with him, talking all the while, for about 15 minutes. He tries to wear himself out doing it. We went in the kitchen and he ate a bowl of cereal and went back to the couch, his tummy full, tired from walking. It took until 4:30 but then we slept fairly well.

Today John had even more **trouble holding his spoon and fork**. He **can't see what he's putting on the utensil** when he uses his right hand, plus it's getting lazier. It's equivalent to using his left hand; the right is weak and the left is not used to being utilized. It takes him a long time to eat a meal. But eat, he can.

One of the "Grandmas" down the street came over with a couple from church. They brought pound cake, slices from two kinds of fruit cakes, candy, fudge, cookies, pecans, oranges, pickles, and chicken tetrazzini. John hit the chicken three times today and has eaten three oranges, although I have to peel them.

I spent several hours in the yard today for the first time in a while. It felt wonderful to cut limbs, pull weeds, mulch leaves and put them in beds. The weather was cool and slightly overcast. Perfect for yard work. The neighborhood animals passed through at some point. The dogs were looking for John because he gives them treats, and gave up on me pretty quickly.

Had my first really good cry. Hospice gave us a book about the steps of dying and at the end is a short piece about how death is like a ship disappearing from your view over the horizon. It's still there for someone else to see, carrying its cargo just as it was when you last saw it, but it's now out of *your* sight. John keeps telling me that, and I know it because all people will live forevermore, either with God or separated from Him, but living nonetheless. I will see John again one day. I don't want him to go at all. He's snoring on the couch right now and it's music to my ears. Looking forward to going to my parents' tomorrow for Christmas and spending the night with everyone. Won't be spending the night with Marshall tonight as I always have, but that's okay. Next year.

December 27, 2010   snowy Sunday, mellow Monday/LC blog
Christmas at my parents' was great fun as always. My sister and her family beat us out there because John wanted to be clean and not gross to everyone. We washed his hair, bathed, shaved, and packed, including our Hospice **comfort kit**. Got a thoughtful call from one of our high school classmates checking on us. Only John and I spent the night with my parents.

In the night, John woke up with a **headache**. He went into the next room and sat in a chair for a while. Being the tough dude he is, he wouldn't take pain meds. It got so bad, he finally broke down and took ¼ of a **pain pill**. Half an hour later he took another quarter pill. Nothing was helping. After a while, ½ a tablet more, accompanied by vomiting. Morning came, along with snow. The flakes were large and swirled in the wind. Mama and I went outside and the dog had snowflakes on her fur. It snowed for over an hour. During that time, I called Hospice and the nurse was on her way. She ended up in Georgia because GPS sends you on an incorrect route through the woods on an imaginary road to my parents' neighborhood. When she finally found us, with Mama meeting her at the main road, John had fallen asleep. While the nurse was there, we changed his bandage. The tumor had grown and the bulge was touching the back of his ear. This was new. There was a lot of yellow drainage. I've noticed that when he has headaches, the next time we change his bandage, there's more yellow than usual.

The nurse thinks it's puss and not brain fluid. The stitch bled more and made a mess. She taught me how to give John **liquid morphine** and what pills to give him for nausea. He took one and it helped for a while. He didn't want morphine and chose to keep taking the pain med Dr. Chemo gave us. I think John has a mental block against the "**comfort kit**" of meds from Hospice because those are for "end of life" and he knows he's not there yet. He wants to be but every nurse that sees him says he's not.

Daddy went to our house and plugged in the heater in the van so the tubes to the carpet cleaning machine wouldn't freeze, and dripped faucets inside the house because it was cold and getting colder. John wanted desperately to go home. I figured it was because he knew it was going to be in the 20's at night and the van heater needed to be turned on. When I told him Daddy already plugged it in, John said, "I guess we can stay another night then."

He slept better, got up at 3:30 p.m. to eat cereal and take more pain meds. Got up around 9:00 this morning, ate, lay back down, then got up and started getting dressed. He was READY to get home. We had a quiet day, back to "normal."

Our main Hospice nurse came. John hasn't lost weight, had his usual sense of humor, and when we changed the bandage, the tumor didn't look as large. Two stitches are bleeding. She gave me a "**spill kit**" in case the tumor ruptures, not using those exact words. Don't know if having the kit gives me comfort or fear.

Tonight, our preacher and Sunday school teacher from Havana came by for over an hour. It was a great visit. Very real. John again told them all that matters is knowing Christ and what He did, and trusting Him because we have nothing to offer God to redeem ourselves. He is still eloquent when it comes to God.
very inspiring

December 28, 2010   doing or being?/LC blog

John made me stop today and lay with him on the couch. It was nice. Sometimes I get so busy doing things I forget to be with him. I think since we're in the house together and I'm buzzing around, I'm with him. But he doesn't think so. Since he can't read or write anymore, and TV is hard to follow, he's terribly bored. So much so, he's called several friends to talk on the phone as best he can. He enjoys it when his niece calls. And speaking of the kids..............

Tim's family sent us a "junk and love box" for Christmas. It arrived today and John absolutely wore himself out having fun with the contents. For years, John has sent them a junk box for Christmas filled with items he found during the summer cleaning rush, along with new things.

They sent us toilet paper, lotion, books about Idaho, maps, a blanket, "moose poop." The box also included a sweet letter about them being sad this is his last Christmas, and they wanted to send a box to *him*. The kids put in their Christmas stockings filled with stuff they chose: mugs from their town, post cards, hand-drawn pictures/notes, and I got a picture ornament from a kids' meal.

John said it was perfect; the "bestest" Christmas they could ever give him. He called his brother and later his niece called back. John is worn slap out. We took pictures of him/us with the loot and of him in front of the stockings hanging on our mantle.

He now has a headache. Back to reality unfortunately. But it was an excellent break from it.

December 29, 2010   wasting Wednesday/LC blog
We slept fairly well last night. John was awake a lot but stayed quiet in bed, not tossing and turning like usual. He got up ahead of me and made coffee, and when I got up, I knew something wasn't right. His **language** took a dive in the night. He seemed disoriented, kind of like he was after the seizures. He hardly talked at breakfast and couldn't focus well, and was slow with eating.

After pancakes, John said he knew he was acting weird and didn't know why. As the day went on, he slowly got better and perked up. I ran errands for almost three hours. It felt good to be out and about. Didn't feel guilty about leaving John home. He rested and even nuked lunch. I brought him Whataburger, which he ate later.

Spent more time being with John today. He wasn't talkative until 8:00 tonight, and we talked mostly about God and what people believe and is he getting the message out about what Christ has done for us. He is concerned that more people don't know.

I emailed Pastor Bob, our Tallahassee pastor, to see if he'd do the memorial service at Wildwood. The lady buying the business is coming over with her husband tomorrow to check out the equipment and sign the agreement. John is now stressing about every aspect of this. Is he asking too much or too little? Why can't she take the equipment tomorrow? I can't imagine what it's like to be him. He's really dragging his right foot today, especially when he gets tired.

The Hospice music therapist is coming tomorrow. This will probably do me more good than John.

When I asked if we could have everybody over Saturday to celebrate Mama's birthday, John gave me a thumbs-up.

Trying to go to bed earlier in preparation for the sad day I have to go back to work. The last of the pretty leaves are falling off the trees. We're on a warming trend now, thank goodness. Enough of temperatures in the 20's!

December 30, 2010   thriving Thursday/LC blog
tears, tears, and more tears
Selling the business finally hit John last night and he cried for a long time after we went to bed. Once he finished, we both slept well. He got up before me this morning (no surprise) and made coffee. I could hear him sniffling. He told me he already had cereal, so I made myself a couple of fried eggs and sat at the table with him. It was obvious he had been crying for a while.

John admitted selling the business was getting him down, along with other regrets: not saving more money, not doing more to tell people about Jesus; etc. It took another hour or so of talking and crying before he could stop. But when the tears ended, John was himself. He worked through it remarkably well. I told him again how proud I am that he started a business and had it 20 years and worked it until he absolutely couldn't.

We went outside to look at his equipment. It probably helped to see everything, touch it, and tell what piece goes with what. I was surprised at how much I actually knew about the equipment.

Fun, fun, fun! The **Hospice music therapist** came today. She plays guitar and sings. She played "Country Roads" by John Denver. John recognized it. She also did "One Day at a Time" which should be my theme song. I'm jealous because she has the "AFI Top 100 Songs" and it was amazing. I choked up when I saw "Come What May" from the movie "Moulin Rouge." Anyway, we ended up with me on piano and she on guitar, mostly instruments only. Occasionally I'd sing with her. Piano/guitar is an excellent blend. John loved it. She sight-read over my shoulder from my repertoire of church choruses. At the end, we did a horrible rendition of "Singing in the Rain." When we finished, she asked John if he recognized it and he said, "No." We busted out laughing because it's his favorite show tune from childhood. "That bad, huh?" I asked. She'll come again in two weeks.

Then came the time to sell the business. The buyer had everything in order; three copies of all the documents. John had to sign his name a bunch of times and he did pretty well. I grabbed one of our neighbors to witness the signatures. Once the papers were signed, we had a long visit with the family who bought the business.

Many people ask **how I'm doing**. I say "okay" because I'm so busy in the middle of it all. I'll fall apart later, I'm sure. Don't have time now.

Pastor Bob wants to visit next week since I asked if we could have the memorial service at his church. The secretary sent information on what the bereavement committee helps with, facilities, and program printing. That's what I love about that church. It's organized but with heart.

It's been a stress-relieving day.

John's parents are coming Sunday for a week. I'm glad because I'll be able to work another week without taking days. I'm not afraid to leave him by himself yet. Mornings are a challenge though. He's **slow waking up and getting going**, but once he does, he's good. Bored but good. And he **takes rests** when he feels tired, which he used to fight. He **can't wash dishes** anymore. His right hand is not trusty. I've enjoyed our carefree days this holiday. If we had someone to be here when he gets up in the mornings after I go to work, it would be perfect. I'm going to try to line up some of his friends to come during the day, the week after his parents leave, just to visit and chat and maybe bring lunch.

Taking it one week at a time, one day at a time. Trying for more being and less doing.

January 2, 2011   It's a new year/LC blog
Not into saying happy New Year because I know it probably won't be. But I say it because I hope it will be.

It's been quiet and good around here. John's been doing well. It's been warm and we've walked outside several times and sat in the sun. I cleaned up the last of the leaves and finished the weed-eating from a month ago. Yesterday my family came over to celebrate Mama's birthday. I fixed black eyed peas, rice, ham, cornbread, tea, and cookies and ice cream. We had a great time.

John called his father last night to tell him they didn't need to come; he's having good days and can be by himself. His dad said the car was already packed and they were coming. Even though John has good days, there's always the one day he doesn't feel good and they want to be there for that. John gave in and they're on their way this morning.

It started raining yesterday around 2:00, a nice steady rain. This morning it's overcast and drippy. Wanted to go to church but John is having some pain and his patch has a lot of yellow drainage again. There is a definite correlation to the drain and pain.

We had a "first" the other night. It actually happened a little at my parents' at Christmas, but this was the worse so far. John **missed the toilet** totally while urinating and soaked the trash can, floor, and rug instead. I'm learning that when I hear, "Laura, I'm so sorry," he's messed up something. We've decided he will **sit to urinate** from now on. He couldn't see the toilet and was guessing he was hitting it. I think he may be losing more vision field.

No accidents since then. Except for the antique pitcher lid. My fault for leaving it in his medicine area on the kitchen counter, and on the right side. It's previous owner used the pitcher for bacon grease. It's tall and slender, pottery, probably from the 1940's. John hit it with his right hand, which he doesn't have a lot of control over. The pitcher part landed in a garbage can below it and the lid went flying and hit the tile floor. Now I can put tall utensils in it.

Friends are coming over this afternoon, but if John keeps feeling yucky, I will call them and reschedule. Don't want to go back to school tomorrow, but thank goodness, it's a planning day. I like hanging out with John. Will have to make a decision about work-- leave of absence, time off.....keep working......

And, with it being the New Year, John's insurance deductible starts over. Will spend most of my day at work tomorrow making phone calls..........thank goodness it's a planning day.

(addition to the previous post)
Our friends understood about not coming over today. John has rested on the couch and felt fine after lunch. His parents got here around 2:00. I fixed dinner—pork chops, Italian green beans, baked potatoes, tea biscuits. We're seeing a **correlation with bad weather** and his head hurting.
rain, pain, drain

January 5, 2011 _____ LC email

I don't have all the details yet, but sometime next week I will be **on leave from school** indefinitely. My friend and fellow teacher reminded me yesterday that we can never have these days back, and my job is truly that--a job.

I have much more peace since making the decision. My administration supports me, as well as my family. The next week will be incredibly hectic as I close out this 9-week period and make plans for a substitute, but it will be worth it.

Thanks for your continued prayers. John smiled when I told him I would be staying home and that sealed it. I'm appreciative of his parents being here this week but the first day back with the students, I knew my mind was at home.

January 6, 2011 _____ fast times/LC blog

Time is flying. John's parents have been here this week. I'm sure they're stir-crazy. They'll leave Saturday. Came to a conclusion yesterday that I should take a leave from work until I'm ready to go back.

John has felt well and done well. A little **weaker on the right side** every day. Pastor Bob came over today to check on us and talk a bit about the memorial service. It was good to see him and talk with him again.

I'm sure I'm leaving out a lot of details of this week, and once I'm home regularly I'll look back and fill in the important gaps.

6 weeks

January 7, 2011   replacement parts/LC blog entry
Met my substitute today and she is delightful. Wasn't expecting
one this quickly and smoothly, but like most steps along this path,
God has orchestrated even the tiniest details.

John's parents will head home in the morning. He'll be home
alone Monday and Tuesday. Should be fine. We'll all call him
regularly. Can't wait to be home. It'll be like having two
summers this year.

January 12, 2011   catching up is hard to do/LC blog
Seems like forever since I've written. Looking forward to getting
in the groove again.

My first day home on leave and it was a busy one. Mama and
Daddy, the Hospice nurse and social worker came by.

John's vitals are still strong. He **drags his right foot** more and has
less control of his right hand/arm. His **right eye is droopy** and
puffy underneath. But he eats good, rests all night usually, and
still cracks wise. Lately, **every noun is the word
"internet"**...literally, especially when he's tired. "Let's take that
internet to the internet."

There is a new part to John's insurance, if we opt in, that would
raise the limit for Hospice care—actually make it unlimited—after
the deductible/out-of pocket- is met. Unless I can get him on
Social Security Disability. Will try to finish the SSD forms
tomorrow.

One more broken item: a glass bottle of makeup remover. John
was putting it back on the bathroom table after his parents left
Saturday. It made a sticky, gooey mess on the tile but it came up
for the most part. Still finding tiny pieces of glass in the corner of
the bathroom.

John's **tumor bulge** is weirder and weirder. It's getting longer, swelling at both ends, with more fluid pockets and one area in the middle of the middle that bleeds when I take the bandage off. Today it looked like there were fewer fluid pockets and that one possibly leaked and is now a caked mess at the bottom of the bulge. Sharon cut his hair Sunday and it's MUCH easier to wash it and pull the bandage off. The last time she cut it, he thought that would be his last haircut ever.
nanny nanny boo boo it wasn't

I'm taking pictures of the bulge every few days. John says I need to sell them one day and make money. I'd like to take my blog posts, email updates, and pictures and write a book about this experience. We've had a lot of questions along the way, most of which received the answer "everyone is different." Imagine a book that walks people through the ups and downs and stages of decline, as well as services available.

John enjoys getting phone calls. He's so bored, even with me here. It's frigid again, in the 20's at night. Tired of it and ready for spring.

January 13, 2011   guys surprise/LC blog
I'm surprised at how many of John's guy friends call him and come by. I am impressed that the men have faithfully emailed, called, and visited regularly. You would think men are unemotional and non-relational, but quite the opposite has been proven around here. Also shows the quality of friends and deep relationships John has.

Yesterday and today, John has had **fewer words**. He is more frustrated that he can't communicate well. He **showed me several things** today when I couldn't understand what he meant. He **walked laps** in the house tonight, which he hasn't done in a long while. I read an article to him about the essential doctrines of Christianity and it got him wound up thinking about God.

John's word retrieval problem prompted me to make a **booklet of pictures** of common items and places. Some of the pictures I included were of diet coke, the coffee maker, bread, the grocery store, pharmacy, church, family members, friends, the Bible; all the things we use or talk about most. It was a huge help in conversation. If John needed to tell me who called or if we were running low on cokes, he could point to the picture. His frustration level went down.

5 weeks
January 14, 2011   cussin' kind of day/LC blog
It began around 1:30 a.m.
I was awakened by a loud **sigh.**
When I dozed off: **sigh.**

This happens when John can't sleep. The last couple of weeks he would **take a P.M. or ibuprophen to relax him to fall back asleep**. For some reason, he wouldn't last night. And just when I dozed off: **sigh.**

Around 6:30 a.m. I asked if he'd like to go to the couch because sometimes he sleeps better there. He must have thought I was SENDING him to the couch because he had a little attitude about it, grabbed his pillow and headed out. Not sure if he slept or not which means he had a rough day. He ate breakfast and lay back down, got up, lay down, back and forth until 11:30 a.m.

I called the accountant Wednesday and he said come Friday (today) to talk about quarterly taxes and answer other questions. I did this in front of John and explained it to him after I got off the phone. He gave me the "thumbs up." But, today, when he reminded me of the appointment and the time grew closer, he lit into me about "how could we expect the accountant to drop whatever he was doing to get the quarterly done while we waited." I explained that we were only dropping things off and asking questions, not waiting for him to do the report today. That appeased John for a few minutes, and then he started in on the "I never tell him anything" and "we shouldn't drop in on the accountant."

John's health insurance company called for the fifth time asking if he wanted the new program that **waives a limit on Hospice coverage** once your deductible and out-of-pocket are met. They are finding it costs the company less and is better for the patient if Hospice services are used instead of sending a person to the hospital constantly as a form of end-of-life care. I have explained this to John a gazillion times, and how we need it. He kept saying we didn't. This, piled on with him being mad about going to the accountant put me over the edge. I told John he was frustrating me. His reply, "You're always right, never wrong, blah, blah, blah." He went to the living room and put his head between his hands and sat for a long time, and wouldn't eat lunch before we left for the meeting. I told him I was sorry. I really did feel guilty for telling him he is frustrating because I can't imagine how frustrated HE must be, not being able to communicate.

He took bananas, water, crackers, and an orange to eat in the car on the way to the accountant.

John's medicine had no more refills and they are going to call the doctor for more. Finally got home, ate, and went to town to fax John's insurance permission to opt-in for the extra Hospice coverage because the accountant told John it sounded good to him.

Now John's head hurts but he's been asleep since 9 p.m. He went to bed around 6:00 but couldn't sleep. I lay with him and while we talked, he said, "I know you're hurting. Tell me what you think." I told him again that I don't want him to go and I'll miss him a lot. He likes it when I tell him that.

January 16, 2011   trending down/LC blog

Saturday was a better day after the trauma Friday. John has less ability with his right side and **lays his hand in his plate** and doesn't even know it. He has mentioned for a while now that he can't "hear" me on that side, and I take it to mean he doesn't have much feeling there. He **almost fell over** a couple times while walking, too.

Today it's been about the same. He doesn't understand why he can't go on and die since he "can't do anything." He lies around more out of boredom, listens to his Bible on CD, and watches TV a little. Late this afternoon, a couple from church brought over homemade pork loin BBQ.

This is what we need from Hospice: someone to teach John **how to get up from sitting** since his side is weak; **how to use utensils with his left hand** or strategies with other types of utensils/bowls/plates; **how to get up if he falls**. I also need to know these things and didn't realize how quickly we'd need this information. **You don't know that you need to ask for these things until you're flailing in the thick of it.**

John has always **weighed himself** at the grocery store and when this whole ordeal began, he weighed about 235 pounds. At the doctor in October, he weighed 209, and this past Friday, 201. He still has his stomach pooch, but his legs are thinner than I've ever seen. He looks great on the whole.

There have been a few moments lately when shear panic have hit me: very soon, John won't be here anymore. It's surreal. I don't like it at all and I told him again.

The Golden Globes are on tonight and I told John several days ago I wanted to see them. My carnal indulgence. He had a chill about 15 minutes before the program was to start. He drank water with his medication and it made him cold. I lay in the bed with him while he warmed up, and he told me not to forget my program. I stayed in bed with him but he said I needed things to do, it was okay. It was like he was saying, your life is going on, and you have things to do. Don't stop them for me. It was sweet.

We've taken pictures of the incision area all along the way. In the picture from early November, the bulge is nothing compared to

today. We thought it was big then. The pictures, especially the
latest ones, are not for the faint of heart.

Months ago, John made his own DVD "movie" for the memorial
service. We've made so many more pictures since then, I made
my own movie yesterday. Now to find the right song....................

January 16, 2011   steps/LC blog
What is it.....five **steps you go through when someone dies**?
Guess the denial has been until now. Not so much actual denial
but maybe not realization. John has been so "normal" until
recently. Now I'm getting angry. Why does this have to happen?
To him? It's not fair. I don't want him to go. Why now?

I hope I get through this stage quickly because I don't like it. Nor
do I want to spend energy being mad.

January 17, 2011   the games of life/LC blog
John's incision bled in the night, that one spot that bled a couple of
days ago. I knew he was concerned because he wanted me to call
the Hospice nurse. I left a message for her, then canceled my
dentist appointment for today, and called Mama to not come sit
with John for my appointment. We changed his bandage after
breakfast and it hadn't bled anymore. The nurse told me to use
two bandages or a bandage with gauze on the outside, along with
the headband he uses to hold it all on.

While I talked to the nurse, John called his fellow carpet cleaner
and longtime friend in Atlanta. Dave and his wife are coming here
in early March. John said if he's already gone, for them to come
see me. Talking energized John. He had a great morning once he
ate and took his regular meds.

What do you get when you cross charades with pictionary, map
quest, what's my line and the internet???? Two hours with John,

trying to figure out the name of a store. The clues were: internet, national store but only one site locally, we've been there a thousand times, he'd go to one side and I'd go to my pictures, near Governor's Square, had other small stores next to it. I finally called Sharon and gave her the clues. At one point, John kept saying Tennessee Street, but Sharon and I figured that was not right. I was pulling up store logos online to eliminate all food-related places, Barnes & Noble, K-Mart, the party store, Tallahassee Mall. Sharon called back about half an hour later with Best Buy. BINGO!! Ding, ding, ding. We have a winner. John recognized the name when I said it. Sharon was cracking up on the other end..... "Thank you very much," John said. I pulled up their website and he confirmed Best Buy was the store. And all the clues fit perfectly, of course............ John wants me to get a new computer and wanted us to look at them online. He wanted to enjoy me looking for one. At Best Buy, he would always look at the cameras and computers and I would find a DVD to buy, which is why he said I went to my pictures. I added a picture of the Best Buy logo to his communication pictures.

Before we ate supper, John prayed. He thanked God for all He's done for us, thanked Him that we can know Him, and asked God to look out for me. We both lost it. John is incredibly thoughtful and sweet.

After supper, John lay down, slept a bit, and then woke up restless. He tried to tell me something he said he's told me twice before. I couldn't figure out if it was about the PO Box, medicine, insurance, or Hospice. He assured me it wasn't me; it's his **lack of communication that frustrates him**. John got up and walked around in the house and went to sleep.

Found the song to put to my video of pictures of us: "Mrs. Darcy" from "Pride and Prejudice." This summer, John watched the movie with me, and I wasn't sure how much he followed it. At the end when Mr. Darcy asks what he should call Lizzie and she says Mrs. Darcy only when he's deliriously happy, John kissed me and said, "Mrs. Cogdill, Mrs. Cogdill." He "got" that part. The song doesn't fit a guy video, but it's perfect to me.

1 month

January 19, 2011   dropsy turvy Tuesday/LC blog

I'm finding that if I don't write each night, I forget what I wanted to say. Yesterday, Tuesday, it seemed like all I did was **clean up spills**. John knocked over a soda on the coffee table and it ran down onto magazines, photos, and books, to the rug. He did a good job getting most of it up and didn't ask for help. We were able to save everything.

Later in the evening, John was pulling back the bed covers and had a stadium cup of water in his....right hand. The next thing I knew, drip, splash. John's hand slacked and he didn't know he was pouring water into the bed. When I called his name and he turned to me, the water continued to pour on the rug and floor. He stood in it in his sock feet. I ran to the bathroom and grabbed a towel and soaked up as much as I could, pulled the covers away, separated the wet sheets. I didn't know whether to laugh or cry. I was mad at myself for being mad at him. He couldn't help it. But after everything was back to normal, I told him **no more cups without lids**.

We walked a block to where the dogs live. They were out. Thank goodness I remembered the doggie treats.

A different Hospice nurse came today. She measured the bulge. Best we could estimate, it was eight inches long. I asked **how he is to stand** since one side is weak. He should put his **weight on his left/good side when getting up and going up stairs**.

John **doesn't try to use his right hand when eating** any more and meals go better because he isn't struggling over which hand to use. When he's tired, the right side of his body droops.

January 19, 2011   PJ day/LC blog

At 2 p.m. I switched my pajama bottoms for sweat pants and pulled a sweat shirt over the PJ top to walk to the mail box. Never did get dressed today. Mama came by for a few minutes. Sat on the couch with John most of the day. I asked him if, when he gets to heaven, **will he ask God** why he got sick, what caused the tumor or anything like that. John said he hadn't thought about it but probably not. It won't matter then and he only wants to see God and talk about Him, but he would think about my question.

The orioles are here, swarming the neighborhood and stripping trees of berries and seeds. This morning we watched them and a woodpecker, red bird, and mocking bird.

John's father is in the hospital in Daytona. He isn't making enough white blood cells. They are running tests and he'll be in until they figure it out and get things under control.

Tomorrow, another of John's friends is to visit us. Another guy.

January 20, 2011   not much new/LC blog

Our friend who married us at Oven Park, brought Chinese for lunch. He is going to come again next week and bring another of John's colleagues. I'm going to cook for them. As John told him, "This is her life," meaning I enjoy cooking for people.

Chilly, overcast day. I ordered the DVD "Jane Eyre" with Joan Fontaine and Orson Wells and it arrived today. John sat through the whole movie with me. He went to bed at 7:30 p.m. and will be up at midnight wide awake. Hope it's not one of those nights.

John tried sleeping on the couch last night to keep his **head propped up** but after he slept for an hour, woke up and saw me still watching TV, he went to bed and slept well.

January 22, 2011   great guys/LC blog

What a random day. John got off to a slow start. At almost lunch time, I decided to get a shower. Of course, when I turned on the water, the phone rang. It was a friend I hadn't talked to in a while.

I turned the water off because I knew it would be a long conversation. About the time we finished talking, a friend of John's called to see about coming over. Back to the bathroom to put away everything for my shower and try again later. We had a great visit for about two hours. The guys talked about God.

Not long after, our high school friend called to find out if he could come over. He did, and we had good conversation mostly about God and the Bible. John interjected some but mostly listened.

Tim's mother-in-law, Georgena, wants to come over tomorrow. I told John he's a celebrity with all these people wanting to see him. He smiled.

We went through his mail at 9:30 p.m. because he was wide awake and we hadn't had time to do it before. John was more "with it" as the afternoon went on.

The right side of his **face is droopier and expresses less**. Sometimes only the left side of his face smiles.

When people call, John **knows their voice** and who they are but can't tell you their name.

January 24, 2011   and don't call me mom/LC blog
Learned a good lesson today. Usually I take my clothes with me in the bathroom when I get a shower, but not this morning. It was not as cold and I took only my underwear. No sooner had the shower cut off than I heard a knock at the front door. I was trapped because John let them in. Fortunately I recognized the voice as one of my retired teacher friends--female. I called her name and told her honestly: just got out of the shower, running to my room. Take things with you when bathing because these days, you never know.

Mama stayed with John while I ran errands. The teacher friend who popped in this morning came back with a spaghetti/salad dinner. She and another retired teacher and I are planning lunch the first week of February. Can you believe February is almost here?

Yesterday and today John's right side has been very weak. Tonight he finally **went down on his knees** in the bathroom. I knew this was coming. He didn't fall, just went down slowly. He told me to go away when I started walking over to him. I watched from a distance. He got up and brushed his teeth. The Hospice nurse is coming tomorrow. I'll call her and see if we can get **a walker**.

I used to think in quarters/three months, because that's about how often John had MRIs. Then it was months; how many months since his last surgery. And suddenly, how many months does he have left. Looking back over the last month, I'm amazed at his decline, and looking at the past week, I'm even more amazed. I know soon it will be days compared to days. Month compared to month, week compared to week, days compared to days. liquidating life

Didn't get any updates on John's dad today. Must not be anything new.
When John is really weary, he calls me mom. I said, "Laura" when he did it today. His reply was, "I know. That's what I said." At least it's correct in his head.

January 25, 2011   marker day/LC blog
There will be days when I look back on it all, where I will see turns and changes. Today will be one of those days. It started out with John a little weak. He ate, sat on the couch, and then said he needed to go back to bed. Not sure if he slept.

A teacher friend called and wanted to drop by soup she made. We had a good visit. It was interesting to hear what was going on at school, but more in an observer roll and to leave it at the table when we got up.

John wanted me in the room with him. His **head hurt**. I pulled in a rocking chair, a bowl of soup, a book, the phone, and a radio with ear buds and hunkered down. I'm learning to **not ask John if he wants or needs something**. I **tell him** I'm going to do it or get it. As with his lunch, when I asked if he wanted to eat, with stomach growling, he said no. I couldn't take the stomach sounds any more and told him I was going to fix him a bowl of soup. He ate it with several bites of French bread.

I read 2 Corinthians to him. He enjoys me reading the Bible to him, and I love doing it, for him and for me. Amazing how many scriptures deal with death, comfort, and hope.

I called the Hospice nurse and social worker and asked them not to come today. John didn't feel like being observed, talked to, or measured. I told the nurse we're ready for a **walker**. She said she'd order one through the company they use but didn't know when it would be delivered. By then, John was asleep again. Not much later, I heard a vehicle out front and there was his walker. The guy showed me how to work it and suggested I **put tennis balls on the legs** since we have hardwood floors. As expected, John said he wouldn't need the walker.

While John was in the bathroom, Pastor Eric, our Havana preacher, came by. He and I were in the living room when John tried to get up from the toilet. He **went to his knees**. I called from the hall but he told me to go away; he'd be okay. I stood there and could hear him trying to get up, bumping into the cabinet, wearing himself out. He wouldn't let me come in and help. I went back to the living room when I heard the door open. John went back to bed, giving his apologies to the preacher. When John walked away I said,
"This is where we are right now. New today. A marker day."
The preacher gave me excellent advice. It was probably a good thing John went back to bed so I could be reminded of things I'm learning the hard way. I told him I sometimes **feel guilty** for having a friend over or going to town because John can't go or always enjoy a visit. He said to **give myself permission** to take time for me. If I'm not fed, rested, or well, I can't take care of

John. Take five or ten minutes to pull weeds in the yard or bake
something, whatever is therapy for me. Grab a neighbor walking
by and ask them to sit with John for a few minutes while I run to
the dollar store or take a walk around the block. He kept using the
word "**caretaker.**"

I have always disliked that word. But I am a caretaker. It was a
hard day for me when I realized that. After John's first surgery, a
friend handed me a card with a caretaker's prayer. I wondered
why she was giving it to me because I wasn't a caretaker. But
standing in the hall at church, I realized I was. The dreaded word
meant for old people. Not me.

At dinner, John and I ate in the living room on the couch. We
watched only a few minutes of TV and he was ready for bed. His
head hurt terribly. He took two P.M.s and finally fell asleep.
While we lay there, I reminded him of things we'd done together
over the years, like driving to Jacksonville to buy books and CDs
at the discount Christian book store and eating lunch at the chuck
wagon place. Hiking lots of trails around here; walking the dry
lakebed of Cascade Lake, then canoeing it when it filled up again.
Visiting his oldest niece and nephew when they lived here. John
would smile and said he remembered.

He did **use the walker to get out of bed** twice. It gives him
something to lean on. The bathroom doorway isn't wide enough to
fit the walker through, and that's where we need it most.   I turned
it sideways and he used it to get off the toilet. Not a perfect system
but he saw how it helped. I **took up the rug** in the hall and
bathroom. Not going to give him a choice about using the walker.
We're there.

Another step down the slippery slope of liquidating life.

January 27, 2011 _____ LC email
Every week brings more decline. We got a walker this week. John doesn't want to use it, but has a few times when he was tired. Hardly any sentences make sense.

John's dad does have leukemia and there are no treatments, only blood transfusions. They've given him "months" to live.

January 27, 2011 _____ the days are just packed/LC blog
John woke up feeling fine the day after the headache. He didn't use his walker; said he didn't need it. Our two friends came for a home cooked lunch.

Mama also came by. John enjoys her visits. Our Hospice nurse popped in with supplies and checked John's vitals. He was wiped out from our lunch company. I told the nurse I was going to buy a **shower chair** rather than get one from them. It's something I can store in the attic easily enough for the next person who may need it. She suggested we check a thrift store for one.

A couple from church brought a big bowl of stew.

Our Sunday school teacher brought diet cokes for John. He stayed a bit and we talked about computers. I baked cookies because my teacher buddy, Sarah, was coming after school. She stayed for a supper of stew and cornbread. It was great to see her and get caught up on everybody. I told her we should make it a weekly date.

therapy for us both

John's father has some other disease along with the leukemia, and if they treat one, the other will kill him. All they can offer is blood transfusions and shots to build his blood when he feels bad. He went home from the hospital today but has to wear a mask when in public. This adds another layer to the surreal life we already lead.

Our Godby graduates have started a Facebook page for Cougar Angels; those who have passed away. The list is too long. And growing.

3 weeks
<u>January 29, 2011</u>   <u>grand central station/LC blog</u>
John went with me to the grocery store to pick up his anti-seizure medicine. I didn't realize he was going in or I would have parked closer. He did great, though. Weighs 196 pounds. On the way home, we visited a couple who has been a customer of John's for years. She fixed snacks for us but John was so exhausted we didn't stay long. She bagged up the snacks for our lunch later.

John took a nap as soon as we got home, then we ate and played with the neighborhood dogs. I did laundry while he napped again. Friends from our Tallahassee church came over late in the afternoon. She and I went to the local grocery to get bread and jelly. John eats four pieces of toast with peanut butter and jelly every morning. The men had actual conversation while we women sat in the kitchen. As long as you stay on topic, you can follow the conversation with John fairly well.

It was another good, fun, full day.

<u>January 30, 2011</u>   45th post/LC blog
I don't know how to describe today. We filled out quarterly forms and John had to sign papers. It's torturous to watch him **sign his name**. He leaves out letters, prints instead of cursive, and when he says each letter out loud, he names them incorrectly. When he finished, he went for a nap.

Several friends brought chicken, spinach, and mac & cheese. After they left, John was **restless** the whole afternoon and couldn't settle down even when he laid in bed. He kept getting up trying to tell me something. Of course I couldn't understand, and he couldn't understand why I couldn't understand. After almost three hours of this, I finally figured out what bothered him. He thought one of the bills he paid wasn't made out correctly. Once we got it all straight, John calmed down and seemed "normal" again. I told him during the middle of it that he was acting weird. I hoped and prayed he wasn't going nuts like he did in May. I guess the bill issued was weighing on his mind too much.

Going to the Post Office today was his second outing in two days. It wears him out completely, but he insists.

Haven't heard from his parents today, but talked to his mom a couple of days ago.

Trying to go to bed earlier. 1:30 a.m. is too late. I will have to return to work one day and don't want to be in the bad habit of staying up tooooooo late.

Hospice music therapist tomorrow!

19 days
January 31, 2011   crash bang/LC blog
John took his **first real fall** this morning. He's okay.
He was on the couch, got up and turned around to get his pillow. I was on the toilet of course, and the next thing I heard was several things falling to the floor and finally an "oomph." I rushed into the living room. John's head was almost behind the TV table, the TV was almost on the floor in the opposite direction, the plugs had been knocked out of the socket, and I'm not sure what else.

John scraped his forearm on something. It barely broke the skin but there's a **knot on his wrist bone**. He rolled over and **lay on the floor** for a while. I put his pillow under his head. After he calmed down, he got up and went to bed.

Later when I asked what happened, John said, "You know the car over there (his walker)....the people in it did it to me (the wheels/legs)." It took everything I had not to burst out laughing. The walker stays in front of the fireplace and I guess he dragged his foot into it and got tangled up.

I had to throw away the two multi-pronged outlets the TV and other things were plugged in to. The prongs were bent. John's arm must have taken them down. Nothing else was broken and his head was okay.

Another great jam session with the Hospice music therapist. John recognized most of the songs.

We went to the bank and cell phone company. He rested again then went out and sat with the neighbor's dogs.

It's been quite the day once again.

February 1, 2011   Tuesday Tuesday Tuesday/LC blog
As usual anymore, I was running late this morning when Mama got here. I had an 11:15 appointment for my "head shot" for the Tallahassee Magazine Springtime quote contest I won, or am one of several winners. It was 11:17 when I went through their door. Thought it would be a receptionist with a pocket digital camera, but it was a real photographer with the whole shooting match. He told jokes the entire time and took about 15 shots. I kept closing my eyes because the batteries in the camera were low, and by the time he'd click, it was time to blink again. He said, "Don't you know I charge $20 every time you close your eyes?" I opened my eyes wide and kept them open. He said, "No, no! Don't do that." He was a hoot. It was great fun.

I ran errands. Have put only 100 miles on my car in over two weeks. Usually I put that much on going back and forth to work in a week.

Mama brought us a chicken pot pie. Yummy. Nothing exciting the rest of the day. Last night we stayed up until 11 p.m. watching John Wayne in "The Cowboys." John liked it and followed it well.

John **flinches when he touches his right forearm** on the table or if I touch it. I told the nurse about his fall. She'll check it out when she comes in a day or two. It's bruised but he moves it. John got around fairly well today. If I change the heater one degree, he can tell. It's been near 70 degrees outside for a couple of days but the heat runs and runs. Tried bumping it down a degree or two, but within a few hours, John said he was **freezing**. I put the thermostat back where it's been. He's good now.

17 days
February 2, 2011   red flags are flying/LC blog
another marker day
John has had a harder time getting around. His **gait is off** and his **right foot barely comes off the floor**. He's also **slept most of the day**. This is a first. breakfast/TV/nap/lunch/nap/visit with Mama/nap/dinner/news/nap/TV/bed
And this is snoring sleep, not resting with his eyes closed.

The nurse came this morning. John's blood pressure was 130/80, lungs clear. She was surprised how large the bulge has grown. We think a **detachable shower head** would help along with the shower chair. She will bring one tomorrow along with larger non-stick pads.

I also asked for a **handicap parking permit**. John agreed we walked too far at the grocery store the other day.
Interesting side note: temporary car tags are $15; permanent ones are free.

A long-time church friend brought us eggs and muffins. Mama visited for a few hours. She asked John if he ever used his walker and he told her no but he might need it one day.
Sooner than we all know.

February 4, 2011   walker, shuffle, march/LC blog
Yesterday was a better day. John got around by himself quite well
and stayed awake most of the day. The nurse dropped off a shower
head and we gave it a try. John likes it. We didn't hose down the
bathroom too badly. I've noticed a weird action. When I bathe
John on the left side, his **right hand mimics** my actions, not quite
touching my hand. It's as though his brain knows what that hand
should be doing and does it on auto-pilot. Haven't mentioned it to
him because he doesn't realize he's doing it. Same thing when I
dry him off. And when his **right hand holds something, he
doesn't let go**. He thinks he does but usually I have to pry the
towel, my hand, or hat for instance, from him.

The Chinese shuffle
That's what I call the way John walks when he's tired. Short,
quick steps. His right foot can't go far so the left one doesn't go
far. I remind him to slow down. He'll stop, think about what he's
doing, and go back to "normal." He also **marched with his right
leg** several times and the exaggerated movement kept him from
dragging it. But again, he doesn't remember to do it often.

Rough night
John woke up around 12:30 a.m. with an awful headache. He took
two P.M.s which is odd because he usually fights taking
something. He moaned for about 20 minutes until the pills kicked
in. He **slept but restlessly**. Jumped, pushed, and talked in his
sleep. This morning we had breakfast and I headed to the bath. I
told him "do not get off the couch while I'm in there." Before I
got out, I could hear him snoring. Slept about an hour and a half.
He didn't remember falling asleep and asked how long he slept,
what time it was, but couldn't understand. I ended up telling him
Andy Griffith was over, Family Feud was over, and now it's Let's
Make a Deal.
got that

He likes using the bathroom at the other end of the house. This
means we go through the living room, piano room, kitchen, and
dining room. I believe the reason he prefers this bathroom is
because the sink is in front of the toilet and he can pull himself up

with it. John actually used the walker with me beside him after he woke up and ate again. He kept **straddling the right leg of the walker because he tends to lean that way**. We made it to the dining room and he started leaning over. Almost timber. He sat in a chair for a minute then finished the four steps to the bathroom. Took the walker back to the couch.
much smoother

Now he's asleep in bed at 1:30 p.m. I watched the redwing black birds run the other birds from the feeders. It's been an active bird morning.

John's mom called yesterday and the doctors have given his dad four months. I don't think he'll make it that long. He's going every day this week for the shot that boosts his blood. No transfusions since he was in the hospital. He's weak and sleeps most of the time.
 race to the end for these two

Will this post ever end??
This afternoon, Betsy, who teaches with me and lives in my town, came with a basket of sunshine filled with chocolates and a mini rose bush. There were several cards from friends at school. As we talked, the subject of John falling came up. I told her about the big crash/bang and she said if he ever went down and I couldn't get him up, to call her, and she and her husband would come.

10:15 p.m.: John needs to use the bathroom and chooses the closest one. He also chose to use the walker to get there (when he lets go of it to get to the toilet, he gets extremely wobbly). Tonight he slid right down the wall onto the toilet with pants on. When he tried to get up, he went down to the floor instead. We tried everything to get him up. He started **scooting and rolling himself** back to the bedroom and I thought, "This is getting him to the room but then what?" I couldn't get him to rest and try later. I called Betsy. She was asleep and "disoriented" as she put it later, but true to promise, she and her husband came. By then it was 10:30. Her husband lifted John right up and got him in bed.

Besides it being late, it was raining again. They were gracious and said call if I needed help again.
I am thankful.

2 weeks
February 5, 2011   successful day/LC blog
Breakfast in bed, **higher padded "throne" seat on the toilet**, TV, nap, lunch in bed, nap.
Made a few phone calls and emails and found a **bedside potty chair**. The sweet couple from church who brings food almost every week had an unused chair and brought it over, along with their dog, Bailey, a Shih Tzu. She hopped on the bed with John and gave lots of love.

Gail brought Scooter, her border collie, who liked sitting on the couch with us. John got up for their visit. While Gail was here, Sharon and Marshall came bearing Whataburgers, and Betsy stopped in, too. Sharon changed our **shower curtain** and I **cut the old one to put under a rug under the potty chair**. (Keep **a little water** in the pot. Makes clean-up easier.) We're figuring it out as we go.

John christened the potty chair and can get on it in one step from the bed. He's even amazed at his decline.

He doesn't like wearing glasses but likes looking out our bedroom window to see what is going on. I moved the bird feeder on a shepherd's hook a few feet from the window. The birds eagerly followed the food and are entertainment for John.

What is a day really? John stayed confused today. He asked Sharon what day it was and couldn't believe it was Saturday. It didn't help that Andy Griffith came on in the evening, then NCIS, then 48 Hours Mystery, shows that come on NOT on Saturday. He stayed up until 10 p.m. feeling good.

I **washed John's legs and feet with warm water and rubbed them down with lotion** this morning. It felt great and relaxed him. I did it again when he got in the bed tonight. He could hardly hold his eyes open. Trying to head off the **leg jerks/spasms** he had last night. I can hear him snoring and he didn't take a P.M. yet.

Today has been a good day.

12 days
February 7, 2011   small world/LC blog
Before John got sick, we would bebop to Jacksonville's discount Christian bookstore three hours away, or to Daytona, or the beach to take pictures. We he got sick, Daytona was as far as we went-- six hours--and Cumberland Island at four hours for our honeymoon. We'd go to Monticello 15 or so miles away. Then it was only Havana to Tallahassee 12 miles, and eventually, staying home but walking the neighborhood. Then we stayed in the yard, then only down the driveway. Inside only. Living room and bedroom. I know it will one day whittle down to only the bedroom.
our world is shrinking

The last few nights, John has **kicked, jumped, marched, wiggled, moaned**, and not slept well. It's been hard to tell if he's doing this in his sleep or if he's awake when it happens. He said he slept well last night, but he moved the whole time. I didn't sleep well because every time he moved, I woke up. On the way to the dining room this morning, John got mad at his walker. He was grumpy and still tired from the restless night. At one point, he banged his walker on the floor several times. I told him not to do that. He could be mad but don't do that; it scared me. He later apologized for it. We both took a nap after breakfast. He sat with me in the living room off and on all day. Mama came over and we watched a movie.

Daddy sent over several big **boards to put under the cushions** of the couch where John has wallowed out his side. He loves the addition. It gives him more support when trying to get up.

I got an invitation to my class Valentine party Monday. I sent a favorable reply.

John watched the Superbowl, propped up in bed, diet coke in hand. He uses an **eye patch** sometimes because he ends up closing his right eye to use his left. We enjoyed the commercials especially.

February 8, 2011   forgetting to remember/LC blog
How do you forget how to walk overnight? John **pulls up with his walker and stands** there, looking at his feet. I ask him what's going on and he says he's thinking about what to do. I tell him to take a big step. Sometimes he does. Sometimes it's a short shuffle.

Last night was awful. John didn't sleep at all, which meant I didn't sleep much. His legs jerked, jumped, kicked, and had **spasms all night**. He would sigh and roll over. He even took a total of four P.M.s throughout the night and they didn't faze him. At 4:30 a.m. I finally went to the couch thinking if I gave him the whole bed, he could stretch out and relax. That didn't happen either. He would sit up on the edge of the bed and pull the walker to him. The sound would wake me up. I'd go in to check on him and he'd say he wasn't getting up. This routine went on until daylight. Finally he fell asleep in time for breakfast.

He can get to the bedside potty by himself. Drives me nuts but he does it. He sits there, waiting. **Takes about a minute or so for him to get the flow going**.

After breakfast, he rolled over and slept soundly. Woke up once or twice. Ate lunch, back to sleep. Maybe he was so worn out from the night, he didn't twitch. I took a long bath. The phone rang four times and John never woke. His Hospice nurse came around

2:30. We woke him up and changed his bandage. John is having a **hard time sitting up**. It's as though he's lost his stomach muscles/core and sways and bobs like a drunk. The nurse measured the bulge at over eight inches long and about three inches wide, but it sticks out two inches at least. His **blood pressure was high** for having just woken up. The bottom number was 90. Don't remember the top one.

I bathed him and that was another ordeal. John could hardly sit up on the bath chair. Again, the whole core muscle group almost non-existent. I did a hurry-up bath today. nap

Dinner in the living room
I talked to my sister on the phone, telling her about the nurse checking with Dr. Chemo on getting John something to **help him relax to sleep**. I went to the dining room so he didn't have to hear it again, and when I headed back to the living room, I heard the walker, looked through the doorway, and **John was on the floor** in front of the couch. I got him up fairly quickly and easily. He gets **aggravated with himself**. He wouldn't tell me what happened, but I think he fell asleep and rolled off the couch, or either he was reaching to put his water bottle on the coffee table and fell off the couch. The side of his pajama pants and a spot on the rug were wet. He stayed and watched TV with me until almost 10 p.m. His **legs were beginning to twitch** and move a lot while we sat there. It was a slow process getting back to the bedroom. I'm probably not even going in there tonight. He landed crossways the bed anyway. I can hear him sighing. Not sure if he's asleep or not.

Tomorrow I'm going to lunch with two retired teachers, then other errands. Mama will be with John. I've told her if he falls to call the local police and they'll send someone to pick him up.
not in the usual police way though

10 days

February 9, 2011   transitioning/LC blog

Last night was some better. John slept until 3:30 a.m. but was up the rest of the night with leg jerks. Our Hospice nurse called this morning to say she was ordering the muscle relaxer. I went to lunch with my two teacher friends, and Mama stayed with John. He "unloaded" after **almost three days of no bowel movements**. He **urinated less** today and the **color is almost orange**.

One of the ladies at lunch experienced the loss of her husband to cancer. It was encouraging to see someone who survived the ordeal.

While I ran errands, Mama called to say John was in **extreme pain with his legs**. She rubbed them. Held his hand. He cried. I picked up the new medicine. **I fed him**, literally, and he took the pill. It helped with the pain, but he still jerks. And his **hands shake** like crazy.

Another teacher friend, Cheryl, came bearing key lime pie. John was in bed but about an hour into her visit, decided to join us in the living room. He didn't want help coming in but with me beside and Cheryl behind, about five minutes later, he was on the couch. John was **restless** the whole time. Couldn't get still or comfortable. We put him in a rolling chair and took him back to bed. I noticed his bandage was quite bloody. I decided to phone the Hospice on-call nurse.

The nurse was wonderful. I told her about the hard time John has **trying to walk**, he **gets hot** often, his **urine color, shaking hands and jerking legs**. She said he is **transitioning**. The word hit hard, but with relief. It was good to know. When I asked her about how long he had left, she said "**probably two weeks. Enjoy him while you have him**." She watched me change the bandage. The bleeding had stopped but he still jerked and shook. We gave him one more muscle relaxer. I asked her if I should tell John that he is transitioning. She said if he asked, **tell him what I thought he could handle**. I heard him get up and went in the room. He used the bedside potty and wanted to know why "she" was here. I said mostly for me but to check his head and legs. He reminded me that he wouldn't be here much longer. I told him that was what the nurse said, too. "That's good news," he added.

I'm relieved to know and have a timeframe, even if loose. So thankful Cheryl was here. Her dad died from a brain tumor and she could see the "markers" in John. He's in bed now but still jerking. Doesn't seem to be in pain though.

The nurse is going to talk to our regular nurse about getting John a **hospital bed** and **home health care to bathe him and change his clothes**; etc. I'll be glad for the help. Think he will be, too.

February 10, 2011   two week notice/LC blog

John slept until 4:30 this morning and most of the day. A Hospice nurse made a follow-up visit from last night, and our Havana pastor, my school buddy Sarah, and Mama and Daddy all came by today. Plus, the hospital bed was delivered. I put it next to our bed. Now I can be in the same room with John during the night. He's taken only one muscle relaxer today.

John's **eyes aren't focusing** on much and he's **urinated once**. He's tried three times unsuccessfully.
victory on the fourth try

The pastor had another good suggestion. If I start John **in the hospital bed with the rails up**, he won't wonder later why I start putting them up. If that's how it is at the beginning, there won't be a change later. John only complained about the rails once during the tries to urinate. He would sit on the pot for five minutes, get back in bed for two minutes, get up again and try. After the second time of trying to get up with the rail in the way, he shook it and asked "why." I didn't answer him, just put it down and helped him get up.

For me, there will be two **dreaded markers**. The first is when he can't say "I love you" anymore. In the past week, he has said it correctly about 60% of the time. When he messes up, it's "good morning" or "thank you." Most of the time he knows he's said it wrong, and will grin or roll his eyes. I'll say, "Yeah, that, too."

The other marker is when he won't remember my name. He's called me Mom several times, but it's usually when he's tired. One time I was trying to help him do something and he said, "Mom, Mom, Mom." I replied, "Laura." He said, "I meant please, please, please."
good answer

February 11, 2011   boxers or briefs? depends/LC blog
Woo hoo!
We slept until 4:30 a.m. then until 6:30. It's 9 a.m. now and it's already been a full day. At 6:30, John needed to potty. He sat and sat again but nothing happened. When I started pulling up his pants, he touched them and said something was **jibberish**. I felt them and they were wet.
oh gosh, here we go

We changed him into dry clothes. I asked if he'd like to try one of the pull-ups we had from Christmas. He said we might better. He got in bed and needed to go again. I could tell an urgency so I got him up quickly, and as he was pulling down his pants, he was saying "oh, oh, oh." John was urinating a steady stream as he stood. Luckily, almost every drop landed in the depends.

Cleaned him up again, got back in bed, ate two pieces of toast, and rolled over to sleep. I started on my Valentine cards for the kids but could hardly keep my eyes open. Took a nice nap. John's still snoring.
waiting for the home health lady to call

1 week
February 12, 2011   roller coaster/LC blog

Today is Saturday. Yesterday was Friday. Rough Thursday night, early start to Friday. Back to bed after breakfast. Home health lady came. We enjoyed her very much. She spent a long time working on getting the gunk out of John's hair. Our high school friend visited again. John always livens up when he comes. Mama, our school secretary and her sister kept me company a while, and our pastor and his wife brought a bowl of warm chicken and dumplings.

And it began again. Fidgets, mumbling, leg jerks. Took a pill, then another. Fought the battle for three hours. I called Hospice at 11:30 and within ten minutes, John was finally asleep. The nurse came and took out a relaxer from our "**comfort kit.**" I gave John two doses during the night because he fussed with his legs again. Has slept almost all day. It's 4 p.m. Saturday.

One of the Grandmas from our street brought John a burger and Valentine balloon, and me a flower to put in the yard. Mama is back, and Sharon came to cut John's hair, but he's been asleep the whole time. John's "pull-ups" are not holding the flood of urine. Mama and I changed his clothes and sheets. His home health lady would laugh at the time we had getting the sheets changed with him on them. **Keeping the relaxer in his system** so he'll stay relaxed.

PooPotpouri is a great product for "that" smell. I squirt it in the bedside potty and it covers odors.

John finally woke up tonight around 6:30.
wide awake
He fussed around until time for his medicine. With it he ate a hamburger, banana, cookie, and diet coke. Mama picked up the name brand Depends and it worked much better tonight. He lets out such a flood that the "store brand" wasn't holding it all. We also have **bed pads** from the nurse, which keep things drier under him.

John has **spoken very few words** today. Even awake, he isn't
talking voluntarily. The responses he does give are quiet, short,
and his usual weird language. His eyes focus for the most part, but
when he's about to drift off to sleep, the blank stare comes back.
He **hasn't even tried to get out of bed** today. This is the **first day
he's never gotten up**. Mama and I decided to **not put pajama
bottoms** back on him. It wears out John and me trying to get them
under his bottom after having done the same with the Depends. He
hasn't complained or acknowledged no pants on. Will talk with
the nurse about getting him a **catheter**. She offered it as an option
for "one day" and I know John hates them, but it would save a lot
of grief for us both. The nurse can break the news to him.

When John is awake, he makes sure he can see his picture
communication booklet because I put the picture of him with his
brother's family as the top page. He props the booklet up on a
pillow next to him about an arm's length away and smiles when he
looks at it. He'll look at Marshall's picture and the neighbor's
dogs. The important things.

It's been a quiet, sort of sad day. Another major marker passed.

5 days
February 14, 2011   days/LC blog
Called the nurse to come again Sunday afternoon. The meds
weren't keeping John calm anymore. She started the **morphine
mouth drops and another drug for restlessness**. It's helping.
His **mouth is filmy and his eyes hardly open**. He does nod his
head and give his opinion about tastes and funny things. One of
his long-time customers brought chicken salad, fruit salad,
brownies, and green beans. John **ate a good bit**. Sharon came
over and Mama is staying the night.

Got up during the night Sunday to give John his meds. He slept
rather well. At one point he put his arm around me and opened his
eyes like any normal night. He was especially aware.

Monday morning, today, I called the nurse for a **catheter**. It's wearing out John and me trying to get Depends on him. I also asked the nurse to have the **walker picked up**. She got out **a medicine for the "death rattle" to help calm the congestion at the end**.
just in case

She explained again **the procedure they go through to "pronounce"** and when I wasn't in the room, the nurse told Mama I shouldn't be left alone with John anymore. The shock of finding him gone would be too much for me alone. A church friend is here with me while Mama goes home and changes. Mama will stay through Wednesday night and Sharon will come then. I have an eerie feeling Wednesday will be "the day." Don't know why. John's birthday is Friday. His mom called yesterday and broke down on the phone and had to go.

I went to my class Valentine party. I gave them their cards, a pen, a hug, ate a little snack, collected my gifts and was exhausted.

It's more surreal than ever.

4 days
February 15, 2011   every breath/LC blog
The night went well. I got up to give John his meds every couple of hours. He was restless only once. His mom woke us with her call and there were many for John today.

The nurse checked in and said John's **lungs are clear, his blood pressure high**, quite a bit of **blood in the catheter**, and she expects "the call" from us any time.

John **takes a few breaths then doesn't breathe for ten seconds** or so. Then he'll take a big breath again. She said the intervals of not breathing will increase. He discovered the catheter in the night. If it is in the wrong position, he'll move his leg a lot. He takes his **crushed meds in applesauce** easily.

We've moved the **morphine from every three hours to an hour and a half** because he needs it sooner. One of the Grandmas made a cake and they both brought it over. Our Havana pastor dropped by for a few minutes, and three teacher friends came after school. I napped then read a little while John was awake. His eyes are slits if open at all. I **swab out his mouth** and he likes to bite the sponge to squeeze out the water. Yesterday he **wasn't able to suck the straw** to drink his water, but he swallows well.

Mama spent the night, and will again, along with Sharon. We had local Chinese for dinner. A nice break.

Couldn't wake John for his 9 p.m. meds. Sleeping soundly, steady breaths.

3 days
February 16, 2011   Johnny Applesauce/LC blog
I missed one of John's morphine doses because I slept through it. Around 5 a.m. he got restless and was having leg spasms. I gave him a dose, rubbed his head, arms, hand, and chest for about an hour, and so did Sharon. Another dose and more rubbing. Eventually he fell asleep and I crashed hard. Sharon and Mama stayed up and had coffee, showered, got dressed. Sharon left for work but not before taking pictures of John and me in bed.

It was a good, quiet day. The home health aide gave John his bath. We discovered **compression points** on his elbow and wrist; only red at this point, but tender. Between his middle and ring fingers on his right hand is a red spot, and when she washed between his fingers at that spot, John pulled away and grimaced. This is the arm he doesn't use anymore and has hurt since the crash/bang fall. She was extra careful rinsing and drying his right arm.

I slept a lot while John napped. There were several calls, but Mama answered the phone for me. Daddy came for lunch and again later in the day. Gail dropped off fried chicken livers for dinner.

The nurse said John's **blood pressure** was 160/100, lungs clear, **urine has sediment**, is clear then pink.

John's parents sent him a beautiful bouquet of flowers with three balloons for his birthday on Friday. In the middle of the afternoon, John opened his eyes and tried to talk for about an hour. He gestured, huffed, made faces. It was fun to communicate with him. I told him about things going on in the family. He would look across the room and close his right eye to see how well he could focus with the left, something he used to do to watch TV or see things at a distance.

 I put a "donut" shaped bean-filled **cushion under his hurting elbow**. Mama was standing on the other side of the bed when I lifted John's arm to place the cushion. He glared at her and she said, "I'm not the one doing it."

I think all the action wore him out because for the next three hours, it **was impossible to wake him**. We tried everything: wet rag, putting his good arm in the air, raising and lowering the bed. We'd get one spoonful of applesauce with meds in him and he'd fall asleep. I called hospice to let them know we're having a hard time getting him to swallow the applesauce. The nurse answering the phone said it would be okay for tonight and that our primary nurse would call tomorrow with advice. We've also **doubled the morphine doses** because at the end of the hour, you can tell when it wears off. Getting up every hour tonight will be rough. But you do what you have to do.

Don't know if his alertness today was the "**burst of energy**" people get right before they die. Consensus is that he is hanging on for his birthday Friday.

2 days

February 17, 2011   Thursday morning/LC blog

We slept well. Doubled John's morphine and still give it every
hour. He isn't "waking up" or speaking although when I talk to
him, he'll **raise his eyebrows** and his breathing changes some.
Since he can't swallow the applesauce, we're back to the original
pill crushed in a drop of water under his tongue instead of his
regular seizure medicine in applesauce. The **morphine is liquid.**
We're cutting back on the other two agitation drugs. He drank
quite a bit yesterday so his **cath bag was at 500 ml for the third
day**.

There was a little "scare" in getting his morphine yesterday. On
Tuesday, they put in another order for it because we were going to
run out. Dr. Chemo, who is our prescribing physician still, faxed
the order to our pharmacy at 5:30 p.m.. The pharmacy was
running behind and when I asked about it at 6 p.m., the pharmacist
hadn't realized it was liquid. He didn't have any. Another
pharmacy across town did. He'd have to fill out paperwork to get
the Hospice order transferred there but "if I have to call every
pharmacy in the state of Florida, I'll get you some tomorrow."
Everything was approved and Daddy picked it up on Wednesday
across town.

love John's pharmacist

Thursday p.m.

Giving the **morphine every hour and a half**. Have given two
doses of the **drops to help with congestion**.

This afternoon, John had a couple of **coughing fits** where he
opened his eyes. Almost immediately they rolled back in his head.
He will often wiggle his foot and this morning only, raised his
eyebrows a couple of times. He's been **non-responsive** all day.
The night on-call nurse from last Wednesday came again today.
She helped me change John's bandage, and I'm constantly amazed
at the changes in the bulge.

Daddy was our only visitor today but we've had lots of phone
calls. Haven't wanted to talk to people. Nothing new to say.

Tomorrow is John's birthday.

February 19, 2011   49 and one hour/LC blog

Early yesterday/Friday morning after I gave John his liquid meds, I tried to reposition his head a bit because he had started to lean over. I put the head of his bed down some, and he began to **gag and cough**. Mama grabbed me a mouth swab and I raised the bed. It all cleared up, but I was scared. What if it happened again and I "killed" him?? The next dose I gave slower and kept a close eye on his reaction. Our home health aide arrived to bathe him and I was hesitant to put John through it. I was afraid he'd gag again or his arm/hand would be hurting. I was **exhausted**. Getting up every hour, half-hour, and hour and a half was getting to me. I'd sleep hard between doses but with lots of interruptions.

John's **breathing was loud** and close to sounding like his normal snore, and yet not. The aide felt John and thought he had a fever. Sure enough. The **thermometer read 102**. Our nurse walked in and found me in flux about his bath. They both said it would help John feel better and cool him off.

All went well until they turned him on his side to wash his back. He stopped breathing and when he was trying to breathe, it sounded like he was choking. I was a nervous wreck. They worked quickly and got him on his back. He breathed better. They repositioned him with a pillow under one side and **ice packs** in six places around his body. His temperature was now up to 103. We continued to wash him with cool water. His cath bag emptied 500 ml again.

The Hospice ladies could tell I was stressed and at my limit. The nurse said she would try to get a **crisis care nurse/continuous care** until the end. Since he had a fever, his **heart rate was 179**, and **very little air was actually getting into his lungs**, she could justify constant care.

She couldn't claim "**caretaker fatigue**" as a reason for continuous care. The nurse's job is to get the patient comfortable and then leave. They couldn't stay and stay.

John was breathing clearly since they repositioned him. I stayed in the room with him all the time, and Mama and Sharon were with me. A little later, we got the call that a crisis care nurse would be here at 4 p.m and be relieved by another at 7 p.m. The second nurse would stay all night. We **counted and verified pills** and liquid medicines. John's breathing was hard but regular. Heartbeat/pulse 120+. Nothing in the catheter bag. Temperature coming down. You could **see the rapid heartbeat** vibrating in his midsection. All day, his hands have continued to "**marble**" as the circulation doesn't make it that far anymore. Tiny veins are visible in his fingers and the nurse says they are cold.

John's brother sent him pictures of the kids for his birthday. The package came pretty early this morning. Everyone told him "happy birthday" several times during the day.

I ate in the kitchen while the nurse sat with John. They will now dispense meds, wipe him with cool rags, and monitor everything to give me a break. It was a weird feeling of freedom. The changing of the nurses took place when the second nurse arrived: counting meds, giving information.

The nurse sat at the foot of my bed and used her computer while I dozed. I hope she was playing cards or something fun. She said people in John's condition with only a few **imminent symptoms** could last for days. But I can't. I can't imagine days more of this for him or me. Mama had been with us about a week, and everyone was exhausted.

Midnight came and went. It was officially the day after his birthday.
John's **breaths dropped** from 16 per minute to 11. Around one a.m., the nurse said, "Here we go." John's **breaths slowed, became shallower**, and I could hear **gurgling** between breaths. The sound came from deep within him. It was awful.

1:15 a.m.: Mama came to the doorway. She got Sharon. The nurse started packing up her computer, notebook, and paperwork. fewer breaths

I started counting John's breaths at some point, and made it to 65. I had my left hand under the back of his neck but I couldn't look at him. Every breath was with effort and I thought for sure each one was his last. At 1:24 a.m., she pronounced him gone. There was one more sharp breath that startled me. I yanked my hand away and laughed at my own jumping. What a jokester to the end.

I asked the nurse if she was positive that was the last breath and she assured me it was. His **body may keep making noises** but his heart had definitely stopped. John wanted me to be absolutely positive he was gone when they said it because his biggest fear was for them to think he was dead and him not be.

The nurse told me to do what I said I was going to at this time, and that was to go to the other end of the house while she took care of everything. I was shaking all over. Mama put on a pot of coffee while Sharon talked more to the nurse. The funeral home was called and they said they'd be there within 30 minutes. small town service

The nurse closed the bedroom door and did her thing. A little while later, Sharon came out with a garbage bag. It had the catheter, bag, and bed pad. I told Sharon I'd take it to the outside trash can. The funeral home guys arrived, dressed in suits and ties, looking a little sleepy. I had to walk around the hearse to get to the trash can. Surreal. It was here for John.

I could hear the nurse telling Sharon and Mama to take care of the linens so I wouldn't have to deal with them. She brought in the left-over meds and destroyed them in kitty litter and water. We again had to sign to verify the count and that they were destroyed. Sharon bagged and trashed the linens.

A couple of cups of coffee later, I went to the extra bedroom where Sharon had been, and she and Mama slept in the living room. I slept hard, and when I woke up at one point, a heavy, heavy feeling set in on my chest when I "remembered," but I went back to sleep.

The day has been weirdly quiet. It's like everyone knows to be silent. One phone call, no visits. Sharon and I went to the funeral home to finalize paperwork. Daddy saw Sharon's car there while on the way to my house and stopped.

John should be taken to Gainesville on Monday and they'll let me know that he made it. Eventually he'll be taken to FSU for research.

We picked up lunch at the grocery store deli. Mama finally went home after how many days.....?? Sharon is spending the night. I called John's parents first this morning. Gave Tim an hour or so because of the time difference.

Sharon and I talked about the memorial service and wrote the obituary. Facebook has a lot of wonderful posts about John Dennis.

It's still weird and unreal. I'm ready to be by myself and process.

February 20, 2011   here we go/LC blog
I'm finally by myself. No one else here. It's not the quiet I notice, it's the stillness. No extra noises in the other rooms. No footsteps through the house. I lived alone for 12 or 13 years before John lived here for nine months. It's not like couples who lived together for 50 years and lose a spouse. But it's still obvious John's not here. Such a void. It's more than only the noises. It's HIM that's missing.

I know now why people try to **borrow home health/hospital equipment**. It's probably different for long-term needs, but in our situation, we needed something immediately and only for a short time. When John needed a bedside potty chair, we needed it that day and only used it a couple of weeks.

Sharon spent the night and we both slept hard. We **rearranged my bedroom** last night and adjusted other furniture. This morning we did something scandalous. We went through the Burger King drive-thru in our pajamas. Sharon even got out of the car in her jammies and slippers to get a newspaper.

We knew people would be coming over later. Mama came mid-morning, Daddy for lunch. My sister-in-law's family brought tons of food. The Grandmas did, too. I felt bad because one of my old friends who attends our church, called to see how John was doing. I apologized for not keeping in touch the last few weeks and told her of John's passing. One of our neighbors brought a bouquet of camellias from her yard for me and John. She didn't know either. I assured her we hadn't told people. It happened in the middle of the night and we used these two days to rest. She and her husband didn't know John well but they liked him and could tell he had a sense of humor.

February 21, 2011   hidden messages/LC blog

For several months, John hid sticky love notes to me all over the house. I found a couple of them while he was still mobile, but left them to "find" another time. I found a new one in the basket by my bed which is filled with pens, note pads, a Bible, lotion, flashlight.....all those handy bedside items. In the basket John left a sugar packet from Circle K and on it he wrote "sugar xoxo John." When he worked regularly, he would stop at the Circle K for diet cokes.
how sweet

He wrote a few notes even when he could hardly spell or write. The few he could locate near the end, he showed to my sister. She told me not to get rid of anything, even books, without going through them first. John told me he was glad he made the notes as far back as he did because he could write then.

February 22, 2011   note of the day/LC blog
Today I found one of John's sticky notes in my Bible while
searching for a particular scripture for his memorial service. His
obituary was in the paper today.
looks nice

February 23, 2011   so many plans/LC blog
Walked around the neighborhood with Betsy yesterday and my
hips are sore today. Can tell I've been sitting on my behind for a
month. This morning started with a meeting with Pastor Bob to
plan John's memorial service. Enjoyed talking with him and
remembering times John and I shared. I think the service is going
to be a great tribute to a wonderful, full life.

Mama and I had lunch in Havana. Sarah came over and a few
other teachers came later. You know how it is when a bunch of
teachers get together. We do what we do best: talk.

Pastor Bob suggested I have a scripture verse on the back of the
service program. There are quite a few I could think of and wanted
to find which of them meant the most to John. I got out his Bible
and first checked his notepad stuck inside. Guess what I found.
Another sticky note from him. This one said, "Love ya! John
oooxxxooo 12-1-10." It got me searching the pages for more. On
the dedication page, he wrote, "John & Laura   Love ya!"

One of John's favorite scriptures to read and to have me read to
him was John chapters 12-17. This past December, he told me
why it was so special to him. This was the passage he was
studying the night of his first seizure, and since then, he wasn't
able to read and study it to the extent he desired. At the top of the
page of John 14 he wrote "Love Laura xxooxx."

John took a photograph of a flower in our yard with the digital
camera I got him soon after he quit working. I kept the picture on
my computer lapboard, but he hid it in his Bible and wrote on the
back, "John ooxx."

The scripture I was leaning to most for the program was John 3:16. On that page was another sticky note. "Laura, Christ is Jesus John xxxooo." Definitely the passage we'll put in the program.

Now to get my slideshow/movie to work....................

February 25, 2011   take note/LC blog

No luck on my video. Couldn't get it to transfer to another program. I stayed up until almost 2 a.m. and totally remade it on John's computer. It saved it, played it, but when I tried it today, it was lost. I'm going to set up his computer in the lobby and show my pictures as a slideshow.

I finally found the video John made for his memorial. And boy, am I glad I watched it before the service. He hadn't let me see the ending, and I knew I'd better. There are three versions. The first is incomplete. The second and third are the same song/pictures, but John put a different written message at the end of each. The one I'm using tomorrow says, "I love you, Laura. Remember, God is a personality." He would always remind me God is real with a real personality and character, not a spirit out in the Milky Way somewhere. The other ending was "I love you, Laura. I will be back for my body some day." That phrase may be a little freaky to some at the memorial, but he and I had long talks about how those in Christ will come back with Him one day and our bodies, some how in some form, will be restored.

Today, our classmate, Roger, posted a fabulous video he made with a lot of the same pictures I was using. We'll try to use it in the service.

Wednesday night, I searched a lot of places for "things" to put on the remembrance table at the memorial. In my search, I found several more sticky notes from John. One was in a drawer I hardly ever go in. I stuck it to the outside of the chest of drawers. Another was in a tin of foreign coins and other trinkets from his past. I can't figure out what he wrote except for his name and the xxxxoooo.

The best find so far has been a small flip calendar where John circled his birthday and wrote xxxooo and his name. On a whim, I flipped to my birthday. Sure enough...well, almost. On the September page, he wrote my name at the top and circled a day close to my birth date and Love, John ooooxxxx. In the picture for my month he wrote his name twice and more x's and o's.

1 week passed
February 27, 2011   it's not about me; it's not about you/LC blog
John's memorial was absolutely perfect. The sound man was able to get John's and Roger's videos to work, and everyone who spoke honored John's humor, zest for life, and love of Christ. There were so many people from each aspect of his life: childhood, school, business colleagues and property owners, church. The message resounded: it's not about John or his illness or even his life. It's about God and Christ's redemption available to us as fallen, sinful creatures. Therein lies our hope.

The other night I stared at the stars and wondered where heaven REALLY is. Having seen the documentary on the Hubble Space Telescope and the eons of universes out there, it makes heaven seem almost impossible to find. How can a person take one breath on earth and their next in heaven? These are questions I've pondered before, but now that John is there, it is more urgent for me to find answers. A lot of trust is needed in these concepts. After the memorial, I voiced my "where is heaven" question to a good friend with whom John enjoyed talking about God. My friend thinks heaven is another dimension. I can wrap my mind around that.
good answer

The Whataburgers at the reception were a hit, especially with the guys. And talk about grown men crying....it was touching to see the expression of emotion for how deeply John touched others. My school went above and way beyond in supplying food for the reception.

I'm sure I'll be processing the memorial for a while. It was amazing once again how God orchestrates events to perfection.

March 2, 2011   checklist/LC blog
Thank you notes are like rabbits. They multiply uncontrollably. As soon as I think I've made a dent in them, the list mocks me.

Received ten copies of John's **death certificate**.

A person's handwriting is important, especially after they're gone. It is the essence of them left behind. Like a piece of clothing still holding their smell. It makes it seem as though they're still around. Like they haven't left. Their mark on the world. Proof of their existence.

A couple of days ago, while getting the riding mower ready for another season, I thought about last summer. John was working, slowly but regularly. When I would mow, even if I had my cell with me in my pocket, I couldn't feel it vibrating because of the mower's motion, nor could I hear it because of the noise. To be able to get John's call should he need me, I taped a zip locking bag to the steering wheel and put my cell in it to be able to see the face light up. There was a little lurch of the heart when I realized I didn't need to do that anymore.

One night during the time John used the shower chair to bathe, I set it by the tub while I took a bubble bath. He came in and sat on it, wiggled his fingers in the water looking for the wash cloth. I handed it to him and he washed my back like I did his. When he started to put the rag back in the water, I stuck my foot up for him to wash too. And the other one. He got a thrill out of it. He didn't have a lot of words that night, but I knew he was "paying me back" for all the times I'd bathed him.

Lately, I'm remembering little happenings like this. Something I do or see in the house brings back memories of the goofy things we did together while I've been off work, or as the seasons change now, I think of how it was a year ago.

Start grief counseling with Hospice this Friday.
Friends are still visiting.
great friends

2 weeks passed
March 5, 2011   plodding on/LC blog
Yesterday was my first **grief counseling** session. What is it that as soon as she starts talking, I melt? In a puddle. But in a good, needed way. There are things I'm already doing well. I need to stay open to the idea that if I go back to school and then decide I can't finish, it's okay. She said I'm **not ready for group counseling** because at group, you hear others' stories and problems, and right now, I need to focus on mine. She's right. When people I don't know very well start in on their experiences, I glaze over.

The reason I slept well the first week or so was from **exhaustion**, but now that the major exhaustion is over, **my body thinks it needs to wake up every hour to give medicine**, which is why I wake up a lot in the night. This, too, shall pass. I do need to **get on a regular sleep pattern** close to what I have when I work. As it is now, I can hardly stay up until 11 p.m. because of not getting good sleep the night before. When I try to nap during the day, I usually can't. I rest but not sleep.

It's good I **blog at night** to empty my mind before sleeping. While I'm not working, I'm going to counseling every week.

Worked in the yard three days this week and it felt wonderful. The Bradford pears, camellias, fuscia, and spirea are blooming spectacularly.

March 6, 2011   whelmed/LC blog

I went to my large Tallahassee church this morning and went to the balcony. It was **overwhelming to be in a crowd**. It wasn't interactions that exhausted me. It was the amount of people. Our world dwindled to the point that I hadn't been in crowds for a while. A friend and I went to lunch after church and it wasn't as overwhelming because the crowd wasn't as large, I guess.

This afternoon I **cleaned out the bathroom**. I threw out partially used shampoo samples, old razors of John's and things like that. I set up three boxes: donate to charity, garage sale, Sharon. I think I'll try to do the bedroom next, later in the week, although it has John's clothes. Cleaning the bathroom was overwhelming. This feeling is weird.

Planning a trip to Daytona with Georgena Saturday for the day. Leave early, get home late. John's mother would like me to stay for a few days but I'm not up to it.
not even close

March 9, 2011   drugs/LC blog

Mama and I went to the wash house this morning to get blankets and quilts ready to put away until next fall. This meant I needed to clean out a closet that holds blankets, my scarves and gloves, and our jackets. I keep one of John's work shirts in that closet, which I wore when I worked with him. I'm learning to check all pockets in any piece of his clothing before washing or giving it away. In the pocket of my work shirt, he left a small sticky note to me. "love ya" I also found two melted Jolly Ranchers in a coat. He got them at Dr. Chemo's office one of the last times we went. And I found $5 in another jacket.

Got a few more thank you cards written while we were at the wash house. Every time I do a few, I think of someone else to thank. Not complaining, just amazed.

Emailed administration that I'm planning to go back to work the
week after spring break. Also told them I will need days off when
Mr. John passes. My time off is going fast now. But it will soon
be summer.

March 10, 2011   lost and found/LC blog

A couple of years ago on a trip to Kiev, Ukraine, I picked up a pair
of hand-knitted wool socks for John. He liked wearing them in the
winter because they were so warm, especially while he was sick.
This winter, I sewed a fleece sole to each of them where a couple
of small holes started. When John's parents visited us in
December, the socks disappeared. I was afraid they accidentally
carried them to Daytona, and threw them out not knowing how
special they were.

John and I searched for those socks, high and low, under and
behind furniture, between cushions. A couple of days after John
died, I glanced at the shelf in the top of our closet, and there they
were. Right on top of everything, in plain sight.

If John found them, it would have been while he was still mobile.
You'd think I would've seen the socks in the closet I use every
day, or that he would have told me where he found them.

To me, this is a wonderful mystery I will ask him to explain one
day. If you know the answer, don't tell me.

March 11, 2011   thankful/LC blog

I Peter 3:12 quotes Psalm 34:15: "The eyes of the Lord are on the
righteous, and His ears are open to their prayers;"

This reminds me of God's protection through John's illness. His
being able to find my number in his phone even when he wasn't
aware of what he was doing. When he'd stumble along in the
house or even fall and the left side of his head never hit anything.

Getting him in and out of the tub, and I'm not that strong.
Working long days, determined to uphold promises to customers.

How many thousand prayers did I, and others, offer up for John's
protection as he moved about in constant decline? The Lord's eyes
really are on those who belong to Him.
Thank you, Lord.

March 14, 2011   time change/LC blog

My husband was brilliantly creative. Time changed Saturday
night, and when I took the kitchen clock off the wall to turn the
hands forward, I found a sticky note from John with the Bible
verse that says, "Hear O, Israel, the Lord thy God is one."

It was a good visit with John's parents. Spring breakers and bike
week had traffic heavy in both directions. Mr. John looks like
himself, a little pale, tired, but holding his own. I took them John's
obituary, the memorial service program, and a copy of the pages
from the guestbook.

The sound man from the church called to let me know his
computer lost all video files before he could make a copy of John's
memorial service. He does have an audio of it. I didn't know what
to say. What can you say? I'm going to pick up the audio copy
later in the week.

Two weeks and counting until work.
Still going to grief counseling.
Working in the yard a lot.
good therapy

1 month passed

March 20, 2011   snippets/LC blog

John was creative with graphics and layouts, composing ads, and
even took a couple of graphic design classes. Yesterday, I rifled
through old papers and found a couple of pictures John took of
carpet cleaning products, as though he were working up an ad for
them. I saved an old Valentine his mom made for him in the early
1990's.

I decided to put the sticky notes John has left me in an album and
label them with when and where I find them. I'm afraid if I leave
them in place, I'll forget where they are and throw some out or
have to re-look for them later.

Still writing thank you notes. I can tell I'm working in the yard
because my nails are suffering. **Sleeping** pretty good at night.
Still going to grief counseling.

March 26, 2011   LC blog

My counselor says I should blog more.

I didn't realize how "out of touch" I'd become in those last
months. John liked TV commercials muted. Lately, I've seen
several with the sound on and have been surprised at the music or
conversations, having never heard them.

Going back to work Monday. Planning day. Counseling, massage,
Marshall's ball games all next week. Talk about jumping back in
with both feet.

I feel close to John when I sing/listen to Christian music. He is
WHERE I'm singing about, with God, knowing the mysteries and
glories we only sing about with words we THINK describe heaven,
God, angels. Part of me is here and part of me is there.

I ordered John's **headstone** last week. It's plain but nice.

<u>March 27, 2011</u>   first steps back/LC blog
Went to church this morning. Arrived late and left during the final
prayer. Couldn't sing for crying but it felt good to be there. When
I used to go to church and John stopped going, I would set my cell
phone on the chair next to me so I could see if he called. Another
one of those **things I don't have to do anymore**.

Actually cooked this afternoon: ground venison, mixed with baked
beans and BBQ sauce over cornbread. Will be good for lunches
next week.

Was sad because John isn't here to clean the tile on the kitchen
counter and wall. It's looking rough. But I remembered he left me
the tile cleaner. The only thing I didn't have was the big machine,
and didn't need it. Got busy with a toothbrush after church and it
cleaned up well.

Still have lots of unfinished "business" from John's stuff and/or
mine. Can't think of one thing I've completed, mainly because
you **fill out a form and have to wait**. But work begins tomorrow
and I'll have to juggle phone calls, faxes, emails, letters,
paperwork, and kids.

<u>March 28, 2011</u>   hi ho, hi ho/LC blog
.....it's back to work I go.

Not long after I received my engagement ring, I either used hand
sanitizer or a cleaning product that turned the gold purple. Where
my finger constantly rubs the band, the tarnish came off. Last
week I took it to my favorite jewelry store to be cleaned. I almost
had a meltdown driving toward the store and a hard time giving the
girl my ring. When she needed to take it upstairs to the jeweler, I
waited nervously for her return. She was gone a while, brought it
back to her room to blow it dry, and it was fabulous. The jeweler
sent me a message to NOT do that again. I assured her I wouldn't.
A little while later I made a stop at my bank and the girl
complimented my ring.

felt good

As long as I've known John, when I'd make copies at school, I'd
spend the time talking on the phone with him. One of the **"firsts"**
happened again. I reached for the phone on the wall to call John as
the copy machine whirred along.

One thing I find hard is **coming home to an empty house**. When
we dated, John would always insist I call to let him know I'd
gotten home or wherever I was going, and after we were married,
he was there when I'd get home. (I'm not ready to get another cat
for company.) My way over this hurdle is to **call someone on my
way home** and be talking to them as I go into the house and get
settled and turn on the TV for noise. This system is working well.

April 3, 2011   all over the map/LC blog
When I'm tired, I get emotional. With my first week back at
work, I'm tired. Doesn't help that tomorrow is our 8th anniversary.
John and I always celebrated April 4th as our anniversary and
agreed that no matter what day we were married, we'd continue to
use that date. It was our first kiss, in the parking lot of the bowling
alley. 2003.
so long ago

I've been tired all day. **Not sleeping through the night**. I wake
up around 2:30 for an hour or so then don't feel rested in the
mornings. Taking a P.M. tonight.

How to celebrate our anniversary? Thought about going to the
Build a Bear store and making a boy bear wearing something that
reminds me of John. For four Valentines, he gave me bears.
Would love to find a blue button-down shirt and have it
embroidered like John's uniforms.
decisions decisions

Our **anniversary** was an emotional day. A particular meltdown happened at lunch while Sarah and I talked about teddy bears. She said when you make a bear, they give you a little heart to put inside. I told her I didn't think I could make it through doing that.

During my planning, the teammate who videoed John proposing set the video on my desk. It was almost a year ago when he asked me to marry him.

When I got home from school, I wanted to immerse myself in something of John's. I put on his favorite hat and started the process of putting together his family's memory packets with a copy of the audio from his memorial service. I spent a couple of hours sorting, reading, and remembering. I gathered old cards we'd given each other to put in my keepsake box. One of the cards John gave me on our last anniversary was between surgeries and there were mixed up words. It reminded me of the decline he went through in reading, writing, and speaking.

Today I found a sticky note. It has been a while since I've come across one, and was hoping to. It was in a drawer of my grandmother's old sewing machine, which I don't go in often. It said, "Genesis 1-12 Love ya! John xoxo."
John loved studying those chapters in Genesis and wanted to teach on it. He worked on a lesson plan a couple of years ago, before he got sick.

Tomorrow I would like to go to the bear store and make one so I can put a heart in it. That's more personal than ordering one. I hope they have an outfit.

John's mother has contacted Hospice. I'm glad. They'll give her much-needed help.

Sarah knows a lady who embroiders. I thought about asking her to put John's Angel logo on the bear's shirt, if I could find one.

When I walked into the store this morning, the embroidery lady was shopping with her daughter. What an excellent omen that I would find the right bear. I asked if she'd embroider for me and she agreed.

I found a tan bear, white tennis shoes, white low-top socks, tan shorts, blue shirt, and the kicker--a safari hat. John wore a safari hat the last several years.

To stuff the bear, you step on the pedal to the blower that shoots the stuffing into its body. You also get to pick a plain, satin heart printed with "I love you" or a heart you press that says different things. I took my Sharpie with me to write "Laura & John" on the satin heart, and put it in. I watched another bear builder help a couple of kids with theirs, and they made a wish and a promise before they put their hearts in. This is a ritual in the process of stuffing. My helper asked me if I made a wish. I told her "he knows." And when she pulled the stitches to close the back of the bear, I fell apart. She looked at me sympathetically, and I told her my husband had died, this was his work uniform, and I hoped to make it through without crying. She gave me a hug. I named him John Dennis, and gave it the birth date of April 4, 2011. When I told Sharon I picked our anniversary date for its birthday, she asked, "Which one?" We do have many of special dates to celebrate.

2 months passed
April 18, 2011   It's here/LC blog

John's **headstone was set** last Friday and it's beautiful. I thought
I'd fall apart when I saw it, but it was more of a relief. Now
there's a permanent memorial to him, registered forever in town
records.

April 30, 2011   catching up/LC blog
blog, blog, blog
or blah, blah, blah

Haven't wanted to blog but there's a lot going on in my mind.
Need to back up and try to remember what's gone on.

Easter Saturday was a tough day. I started out working in the yard,
but had **no motivation** or pep. After lunch, I gave in to the feeling

and spent the rest of the afternoon on the couch. Took a cat nap and watched TV. Easter Sunday was special, thinking about John in heaven celebrating his first Easter with Jesus, the reason for our hope. Lunch with the family then home. Put on John's hat and started going through the chest of drawers, getting ready for our upcoming garage sale. I found five sticky notes! One of the funniest places he put a note was in the last pair of his favorite underwear. In a book entitled "A Time of Departing" John highlighted the title page and signed his name with xxoo's. Those words must have resonated with him.

Just as there were **markers of decline** for me to watch for in John, I am discovering what his main marker was for himself—**signing his name**. Going through his office, I've found page after page where John practiced signing his name. I knew he did this when he got ready to sign the photographs he had enlarged for me, but I found pages of practice in notebooks, on scratch pads, and sheets of notebook paper. One of the sticky notes I found was late in the process when he started printing his name and spelling it "Johe."

John's brother, Tim, and a couple of his kids have come from Idaho and arrived in Daytona last night. Mr. John had been in the hospital for several days. Tim helped get him home today and there won't be any more treatments.

May 5, 2011   LC/blog

After school, Sharon, Marshall, and I went to Oven Park to commemorate my first wedding anniversary. The picnic basket was loaded with veggies, fruit, cheese, crackers, and juice. I brought the bear I made in April, and we took pictures around the park. Another couple was getting married at the same spot John and I took our vows. Many wishes for happiness to the young husband and wife.

Later that evening, I found out that Mr. John passed away. He and John Dennis can celebrate our anniversary on the other side.

May 7, 2011   so many firsts/LC blog
Today is Saturday and I'm in Daytona. Mr. John's funeral is
Monday. Tim talked a lot about his dad's final days. It's been a
hard time for them, but it worked out best that he came to help.

At lunch, I noticed how much Tim's arms look like John's. I had a
moment of fighting tears and went out on the deck to process it all.

May 8, 2011   making John proud/LC blog
My goal this weekend is to make John proud and represent him
well. It's Mother's Day.
Tomorrow will be a long, emotional day. I'm taking John's silk
hankie from his wedding tuxedo with me, along with a metal
pocket "stone" with xoxo I gave him. Wanted something of him
with me at the funeral.

4 months passed
June 14, 2011   sizzling summer/LC blog
The school year ended quietly. Visited a **probate lawyer** to help
with closing out John's accounts. Walked at the park tonight. I
think it's the first time without John.
another "first" tackled

June 27, 2011   still hot/LC blog
Counseling is going well, every other or third week. I'm going
through the stages correctly and I'm glad it's summer so I can
continue to rest, recoup, and relax (my 3-R's).

5 months passed

Summer seems to be flying by one day, dragging the next. Guess that averages out to.....average.

Found another sticky note from John. I was in the middle of printing out my whole blog and needed more printer paper. Stuck to the top sheet in the package was his note: "Laura, Ohk   Jet & Laser   John xxxooo"

He always insisted on using 24 pound paper for the laser jet printer and wanted to make sure I remembered.

At John's memorial, our music therapist sang "It Is Well With My Soul." It has been one of the songs for the congregational singing every time I've gone back to my Tallahassee church. I joined the choir at our Havana church and one of the songs we're singing is "It Is Well," my new theme. Pastor Eric has been going through the book of John for several months and has been in chapters 12-15 lately. It's been great to hear about these particular scriptures since they were special to John.

I wonder how many hours John has spent talking theology with St. Paul or Moses or King David.

blows my mind

I took a trip to Idaho to see John's brother and family, with a side trip to Glacier National Park in Montana to visit friends. It was relaxing, cool, and got me moving around some. Resting on the couch for almost a year added the pounds. Couldn't get in shorts and jeans I usually wore.

Idaho was beautiful. Tim's family lives near a large lake with mountains in the distance, green and lush all around. It was emotional but filling to be with them, a part of John. When it came time to leave, it was emotional for us all. I wanted to stay and absorb more John-ness.

Montana had record snowfall winter of 2010-11 and it was still deep when I was there. Got in the middle of a snowball fight at the Continental Divide/Logan Pass, built my traditional snowman, thought about John a lot. One morning I realized he was gone. Truly gone. I couldn't call him or email about the wonderful time I was having out west.

This was my **first trip** without him waiting. I was ready to come home, to surround myself with things of his and get him back in my head.

At the end of September 2011, I went back to Kiev, Ukraine on a mission trip with Music Mission Kiev. It, again, was the **first time** I visited there without John still in the States. The people at the mission knew about his illness and had prayed for us. The widows we work with hugged me a lot and cried. My birthday fell during this trip and they had cake and sang to me. It was good to **have my birthday in not-the-usual way**. It wasn't as glaring that John wasn't there.

When I got home from Kiev, Mama handed me a bag from John. He gave it to her one of those days she sat with him while I ran errands, and made her promise she'd give it to me on my birthday. I messed that up by being gone, but I'm sure he understood. It was a stuffed bear in a party hat that sings "Happy Birthday" and a Hoops & Yoyo singing birthday card I gave him a year ago. I continue to be amazed at his thoughtfulness. It was the perfect surprise.

I continue Hospice grief counseling about every other week. We tried every three weeks but I was a nervous wreck by the third week. Hospice offered one year of counseling and it was a tremendous help. In January, I stopped individual counseling and began group.

John's uncle, his dad's brother, passed away from leukemia. How much is too much??

6 months passed

<u>August, 2011</u>   hair today, gone tomorrow/LC blog

Three and a half years ago, I **cut my hair** and **donated it to Locks of Love** in memory of my "bestest" friend, Vickie, who died of lung cancer. When we realized how sick John was and he shaved his head for surgeries, I decided to grow and donate my hair again. I waited until after my trip west because I knew we'd be hiking and I wanted to be able to put it up. My sister was all too happy to chop-chop the length and ship it off to be made into a wig for someone going through chemo or in need of the hair I could give.

It was another emotional, meaningful connection to John. Everyone in the salon knew why I was there and were encouraging and supportive of my new look. My plan is to grow and donate it again in a couple of years. There are stipulations for donating hair. If you are interested, check with your hair care professional.

7 months passed
September 14, 2011   COM memorial service/LC blog
The second week of September, my friend, Curt, who teaches at
the FSU College of Medicine invited me to the cadaver memorial
service at the school auditorium. "Does this mean John is up to bat
this semester?" I asked. There was a peaceful pause on the other
end then he told me they worked on John over the summer. They
needed one more body at FSU and he was next up specifically for
that school. John made it to college barely under the wire. How
like him. "I would be honored to attend," I said.

If there were any lingering doubts as to whether body donation was
the way to go or not, they melted away after my time with the
students from the classes of 2014 and 2015. I've never been more
sure of anything in my life.

Curt said there would be a parking spot reserved for me. I parked
in the circle and went in the building, after taking pictures of it,
and told them my name. They immediately recognized it,
whispered to each other that I was there for the service, and if I'd
follow the gentleman, he'd direct me where to park. I felt like a
celebrity.

I waited in the lobby until Curt met me. Students set up a
reception table with cupcakes and punch, and scurried around
taking care of last minute details. Curt introduced me to the man
over the department, who used to work at the Anatomical Board. I
was thanked profusely for our donation and especially for being at
the memorial.

As the attendees entered the auditorium, they were handed a black
rubber bracelet that read, "In loving memory of our first patients."
The magnitude of the whole evening was dawning on me. I wore
my bracelet proudly. The program cover said, "In honor of those
who graciously donated their bodies to our medical education,"
with a soft, pale pink rose centered on it. Inside the program was a
list of cadaver numbers assigned by the state, along with the cause
of death and the name of the student who would talk about their
anatomy group experience. It was easy to tell which number was

John's because of the listing of glioblastoma. After each student spoke, they placed a white rose in a vase. By the time all 22 roses were combined, it made a lovely arrangement. The girl representing John, like all the student presenters, talked about the bonding that went on as their group worked on the bodies. Curt told me of his first anatomy group and how he still keeps up with at least one of them. "You never forget it," he said.

In the director's talk, he referenced a family member of one of their cadavers being in the service, and again, his thanks were overflowing.

When the service ended, Curt took me on a tour of the building. It was amazing even to me, a medical-phobic. By the time we made it back to the reception, most of the group had cleared out. He introduced me to a couple of the students and we chatted about the specialties they want to pursue. When they found out I was the family member representing one of the bodies, the thanks poured again. Each spoke of the importance of this first semester of anatomy and the need for that "first patient" to work on. I was impressed and came away confident in the future of medicine.

There was a group of four girls hanging back, watching, hesitant to approach. Curt called them over and amidst the introductions, said my husband was one of the bodies they worked on.

"He had the THING on the side of his head," I told them. They all nodded. I gave a quick version of John's illness and why the tumor grew out like it did. I urged them with questions, and their answers told me what I wondered.

When John's body arrived, all the students had observed the protruding tumor. This is exactly what I wanted to happen. I asked if any of them were interested in neuro, and they told me a couple of the second-year students were. They worked on the back of the bodies, then extremities and abdomen. One of the girls in the group I was talking to explored John's abdomen. The anatomy groups rotated to different bodies as they learned different parts of the anatomy.

"But what about his head?" I kept asking. They looked at each other and whispered, and looked to Curt. He must have given the okay because one of the girls said they kept the brains and would be learning about them this semester. I was thrilled and thanked them for telling me. I'm sure my enthusiasm was unexpected, but this is why we wanted to donate John's body: research, research, research that may keep someone else from dying of GBM one day.

 One of the girls never found her voice in our conversation, overcome with emotion to meet someone who made such a precious donation to their education. She teared up along with me.

The girls and I took pictures in front of the vase of roses and I adopted them in my heart.
Seeing the gratitude of the students and teachers and the need for body donation in their education, I tell anyone considering this avenue to do it. It is a lasting, far-reaching gift. I know it's rare for a family member to attend a "first patient" memorial service. I count it an honor, and will remember it as one of the most amazing events in my life.

I made quick mental calculations. If they received John's body in June and it was returned in August, surely it wouldn't be but a few months at most before his ashes were returned to me.

8 months passed
October 14, 2011   Wally/LC blog
A couple of days ago, Marshall went with me to the Humane Society to **find a cat**. The house had become too still again and I should be done with trips for a while. The lady told me about a cat adopted out by them as a kitten years ago and recently came back starved almost to death. He was well enough to find a home again and would I be interested. Marshall decided Wally had great potential. I signed the papers and went back to pick him up today. He's still gaining weight but is a handsome orange tabby who loves to cuddle. Ah, the pitter patter of paws in the house once more.

And wonderful company to come home to.

John's brother will begin treatments for throat cancer. Again, how much is enough for one family??

9 months passed
November 25, 2011   first Thanksgiving/LC blog

The firsts without a loved one are tough, and there are so many. **Thanksgiving** would be an especially obvious John-void because he could put away some food. And my mother can sure cook it. This year, my sister's in-law family invited our family for lunch. Again, it helped to **celebrate a tradition in a new way** rather than with one less chair around our usual table. It was an enjoyable, relaxing day.

10 months passed
Christmas, 2011   LC blog

I spent Christmas Eve night with my sister's family as I have since Marshall was small, except for last year. It was sad to be without John but fun to be back experiencing the excitement of that special morning. The rest of the holiday was much as usual: time at my parents', opening gifts and eating. My thoughts frequently went back to last Christmas and John sitting in the recliner with the headband holding his bandage in place, snow, and an awful headache the next day. Has it really been a year??

11 months passed
January, 2012   Hospice counseling/LC blog

Individual Hospice counseling has been priceless. Everything I'm feeling is normal, even when my emotions are all over the map. I'm naturally a problem solver and have worked through the "why I'm reacting like this" fairly well. It's time for the 6-week **group counseling**.

I found myself more depressed when I left group than when I arrived. It was overwhelming hearing so many experiences. But I promised my counselor I would do this so each week I went and each week I handled it better. The topics we covered were helpful and a lot of it we talked about in my individual sessions. It was important to hear it again, though. We participated in art and music activities. By the potluck dinner final session, I was finally looking forward to our meetings and didn't want them to end yet. Mama made John's favorite chicken pot pie for me to take to the potluck.

A couple of other ladies in our group, young like me, had lost their husbands. It was comforting to hear they hadn't been able to get rid of particular items belonging to their spouse, too. **Each person's grief is different and never stops. And it's okay. Mentally, I can't handle as much as before. I never know when I'll be overcome with emotion. Feelings and reactions are magnified. I can spend a day on the couch if I need to, but I can't stay. Now that I'm coming out of the "shock" of John's death, it's getting harder because I'm feeling. It was months before I could go to a large store or church without feeling panic from being around so many people. I have limits. I want to hear others talk about John. I have no regrets. It takes a lot of energy to grieve. It's okay to enjoy.**

After the group sessions ended, I had one more individual counseling session for personal closure. I could NOT have made it this far, sane, and in one piece without it.

1 year passed
February 10, 2012   ashes to ashes/LC blog
Friday afternoons at school are for setting up the next week. Unless you get an email that your husband's **ashes have arrived** at the funeral home and are available for pick-up. I couldn't think of anything else. The minute I hung Monday's basics on the board, I headed to the funeral home.

The box was in a nice gift bag and was bigger than I thought it would be. When I got home, I opened the outer box far enough to see John's name on the inner box. I wanted to confirm the package was really his. The box sat on the kitchen counter while I thought about how to proceed. Later in the evening, I set it in his office chair and when I would walk through the room I'd wave at him. John would get a kick out of that.

I finally figured out why John died on the day he did. My thinking was "how cool to die on your birthday, the 18th; a complete circle." But he didn't. It was technically the next day when he stopped breathing.   I forgot his mother's birthday was the 20th. He refused to die on his birthday or hers. He picked the day in the middle. I truly believe John knew exactly what he was doing.

And now I had his ashes and his birthday was the next week. I didn't tell anyone my plan, although my family was fairly sure what I would do. John's 50th birthday was on a stormy Saturday this year, and the one-year anniversary of his death fell the next day. I skipped church and headed to the cemetery. The ground was easy to dig from rain the day before. The sky was clear and the wind blew but it wasn't cold. A beautiful morning. After the fact, I let both our families know it was done. I wanted to do this by myself. Me and God. And John.

All in all, I'm glad it didn't take the full two years to get his ashes back from the Anatomical Board. It was becoming an unfinished detail in the back of my mind. But as with every aspect of my life with John, this, too, was perfect.

Even though I knew I wouldn't be at church that day, I signed up for sanctuary altar flowers in memory of John. My sister put together a gorgeous arrangement that currently sits on my mantle along with a few photographs John took.

13 months passed
March, 2012   getting out of Dodge/LC blog

"You've never visited us here" was all it took for me to secure tickets to Scottsdale, Arizona to visit my friends over spring break. It was a good decision. Sure, I was probably avoiding being at home over spring break, but what a great distraction. I recognized my avoidance and embraced it. Summer would be here soon and I'd have weeks to adjust to being home and find a routine. One week at home seemed harder.

This had to be my last trip for a while. Three major jaunts in one year are fabulous.............but..........

16 months passed
June, 2012   dream come true/LC blog

It really is possible to put my experiences with John into a book to help others. I'm ready for the next phase of this journey to begin. My sadness is not gone and will always be a part of me. I think of John constantly and hope I always do.

John has been gone as many months as he was sick.
His brother is now cancer free!

I've found about two dozen sticky notes hidden around the house. When I think I've found them all, like this past Christmas, six months later I'll find two more. Most of them remind me that John is going to God and he'll see me again one day. One was under the DVD player. Another was in a toy box. On the top shelf in a bathroom closet. In a movie case. I tell myself each is the last, but secretly hope there are more.

Such is the journey in liquidating life.

Post Script

*If you or a family member can **benefit from Hospice services**, contact the organization near you. Guidelines, rules, and laws over Hospice, insurance, and end-of-life care are constantly changing. I don't want our initial frustration with insurance to give anyone hesitation about utilizing this compassionate, crucial support.

*Several things that **helped me deal with the void** after John's death were getting a pet, joining choir, blogging/journaling, counseling/support group, joining brain cancer online groups, picking up my hobbies again.

*Keep a lock of your loved one's hair. Take a picture of their hands. Hands are unique and personal, and hold "touching" memories.

*It is thought the sense of hearing is the last to leave a person. Never stop saying "I love you."

Hints for friends and family
What to do/not do

*When you call to find out if we need anything, **be specific**. If you ask, "Do you need anything?" or say, "Let me know if you need anything" you will probably not be given a task. Instead, try asking, "I'm headed to the grocery store. Do you need milk, too?" "We're going to the store. What kind of soda does John like?" If you bake a batch of cookies or make a pot of soup, just bring some over. We enjoyed "pop-in" visits, but for some, it's not appropriate. If you're not sure, call first. Short visits are best.

* Every **meal brought over** while John was sick meant time I could spend with him and not working in the kitchen. In hindsight, it was more important to have meals before John died than after. It also let him see how much others cared. After his memorial, and out-of-town family left, there was only me in the house, and I didn't eat a lot. Check on dietary restrictions first.

* If you've lost a loved one and you want to tell about it, please don't. We usually can't handle it. Our minds are already so full of medical terms, figuring out when the next dose of meds are due, or wondering if we used the bathroom this morning, one more thought is too much unless we're asking questions and driving the conversation. If our eyes start to glaze or that simulated smile forms, try telling it again after I've walked my journey. Instead, **tell me I'm going to survive this.**

* "I'm sorry for your loss."
Television police dramas from the 1980's gave us these words when we didn't know what to say to someone who experienced the death of a loved one. This phrase, while a good start, is now too trite and over-done. He isn't a loss. He's John. **Say his name**. And if you can't remember or don't know their name, use *husband, wife, friend.*

Instead, you could say, "I'm so sorry to hear about John's passing." "I'm very sorry you have to go through this."

* "You're in my thoughts and prayers."
I love every person who sent a card after John died, but 9 out of 10 closed with this phrase. Some other suggestions are:
"I think of you often."
"I think of you when I see (or hear)....and it reminds me to say a prayer for you."
"I'm praying for God's peace to fill your days."
"Remembering the good times and celebrating John's life...."
Recall a memory you have of the deceased. It makes us glad you remember.
Pick a favorite poem, line from a song, or scripture verse to write in the card.
Make it personal.

* Be understanding if we don't want to go somewhere with you. Some days are good and some aren't. Everything is overwhelming. We may need to come late to a function or leave early to avoid too much mingling.

* We'll tell you when, or if, we're ready to date again, or have another child, or adopt.

* Send cards, emails, or call even months after the funeral. I was touched when several friends sent me cards at the one-year anniversary of John's death. We are remembering days like their birthday, wedding anniversary, or death, and it's comforting to know others are, too.
Even if something silly reminds you of the person, **tell us.**

*Don't be afraid to talk about our loved one because you think it will make us cry. It may, but we'd rather have them remembered than avoided. Again, to know you also think of them means the world to us.

Helpful Websites

American Brain Tumor Association   www.abta.org

National Brain Tumor Society   www.braintumor.org

American Cancer Society   www.cancer.org

Hospice Foundation of America   www.hospicefoundation.org

locate a hospice   www.hospicedirectory.org

Big Bend Hospice   www.bigbendhospice.org

Choose Hope (cancer awareness/support)   www.choosehope.com

Locks of Love (hair donation)   www.locksoflove.org

Laura's Liquidating Life blog   www.liquidatinglife.blogspot.com

John's writings on his beliefs   www.cogdillwritings.blogspot.com

A Tallahassee native who graduated Florida State University,

Laura Cogdill is certified in elementary and primary education and

has taught in these grades for over twenty years.

The Tallahassee Writers Association, where Laura served as

secretary, and the Havana Writers Group, have played an

important role in developing her writing skills.

Laura's yard shows the evidence of her love for gardening. She

also enjoys playing the piano and flute, hiking, and reading.

www.lauragcogdill.com
lauragcogdill@gmail.com

33957724R00093

Made in the USA
Lexington, KY
19 July 2014